Dear CIPP/E student,

This book contains three exams to help you succeed in passing the CIPP/E exam. The exams should help you identify the areas in which you need to improve your knowledge, and should train you to answer all questions within the allowed time.

The exams are followed by an answer key for a quick scoring of your exam. After, the questions are repeated with the correct answer highlighted and explained. This should provide some insight into how questions can be phrased, and the common mistakes to look for.

Take 2.5 hours per exam. You are allowed to return to (unanswered) questions, but only within 2.5 hours. During the exam you will be able to 'flag' questions, so you can return to them easily if you have time left.

If you scored 80% or more on all three exams in this book, you should be ready for the exam!

Sincerely,

Franklin Philips

Exam 1:

1. Several treaties have played an important part in the establishment of the European Union. Which two treaties did the Treaty of Lisbon amend?
   A. The Treaty of Maastricht and the Treaty of Rome
   B. The Treaty of Amsterdam and the Treaty of Madrid
   C. The Treaty of Paris and the Geneva Convention
   D. Directive 95 and the E-Privacy Directive

2. The European Union consists of several institutions and agencies. Which of the following institutions is least involved in the drafting, approval, or monitoring of the GDPR?
   A. The European Data Protection Board
   B. The European Parliament
   C. The European Commission
   D. The European Data Protection Supervisor

3. Several courts are accessible at both a national and an international level. Which court has the final say if a case is taken to a higher court the maximum number of times?
   A. The National Court
   B. The European Data Protection Court
   C. The European Court of Justice
   D. The European Data Protection Board

4. Before the GDPR, there was Directive 95(the Data Protection Directive). Which is the most impactful difference between the GDPR and Directive 95?
   A. The GDPR adequately describes data subjects
   B. Data subjects have gotten the right to access their personal data under the GDPR
   C. Article 82 of the GDPR allows for data protection authorities to issue fines
   D. The GDPR is a Regulation, and the Directive 95 is a Directive

5. Laws in the EU go through a lengthy process, both for its development and approval. Which two EU institutions vote on a law?
   A. The EU Parliament and the Council
   B. The European Court of Auditors and the European Commission
   C. The European Commission and the European Court of Justice
   D. The European Court of Justice and the Council

6. Some more laws and regulations pertain to privacy and data protection, it is not just the GDPR. Which legislation is also referred to as the cookie directive?
   A. The GDPR
   B. An amendment to the e-privacy directive
   C. CAN-SPAM
   D. Directive 95

7. Which of the following is most likely covered by the EU Directive on privacy and electronic communications?
   A. Snail mail marketing
   B. An internet provider's HR records
   C. A retailer's marketing e-mails
   D. Recovery of unencrypted hard drives

8. Personal data can be described as anything that says something about anyone. Which of the following options best fits the definition of personal data?
   A. A single GPS location
   B. A copy of a deleted e-mail with the address removed
   C. The nickname someone uses online, and the data attached to it
   D. Anonymized data about someone's online activity

9. A controller can be an organization that determines the means and purposes of the processing of personal data. Which of the following activities best fits the definition of a controller?
   A. A restaurant only accepts reservations by phone and doesn't use a computerized reservation system
   B. An organization performs data analytics on datasets provided by your organization
   C. A cloud storage provider that offers a certain level of security
   D. A delivery company that processes the list of delivery locations for its corporate customers

10. Not all data should be considered personal data. In which instance is the data most likely not considered personal data?
    A. A series of bank account transactions, with the bank account number and name removed
    B. A dataset processed by a processor, which is not covered by the Data Processing Agreement
    C. A copy of a dataset, with the names not visible on the copy
    D. Publicly available data about someone, not of a sensitive nature

11. It may not always be clear whether a certain way of processing reveals sensitive personal data. Which of the following most likely reveals sensitive personal data?
    A. Someone's bank account balance
    B. A public computer's browsing history
    C. A corrupted hard drive that previously contained sensitive data about someone
    D. A nationality in a passport

12. Open text fields are often used at the end of a survey for information that didn't fit in multiple-choice form. When using an open text field in a company survey, what is a possible negative consequence?
    A. A respondent possibly (mis)uses it to enter sensitive personal data
    B. Consent is required for the processing of the survey
    C. The retention period of the survey will need to be further restricted
    D. A Data Protection Impact Assessment is required

13. Not every process contains personal data. Which of the following is not necessarily considered processing of personal data?
    A. Storing employee self-assessments
    B. Sending paychecks to personal addresses
    C. Requesting someone to provide his/her medical records
    D. Transferring financial data to the tax authorities

14. The GDPR can be applicable in cases you don't expect, especially with the global way of doing business nowadays. To which of the following does the GDPR least likely apply?
    A. A German producer of consumer goods
    B. A non-EU producer selling globally through a local reseller
    C. A Swedish meatball restaurant
    D. A French organization, focusing on data analytics in the US

15. If you are an Australian citizen, when does the GDPR provide protection for the use of your personal data?
    A. When abroad, outside of the EU
    B. When ordering from a German-based global retailer
    C. When working for an Australian company that mainly deals with EU businesses
    D. Hardly ever, Australia is not part of the EU nor does Australia have a treaty with the EU regarding data protection

16. Processing personal data under the GDPR requires a lawful processing criterion to be applicable. Which lawful processing criterion would you use as a retailer to process someone's name & address for shipping the ordered item?
    A. Consent
    B. Necessary for the performance of a contract
    C. Protection of vital interest of the data subject
    D. Necessary for the performance of a public task

17. CIA stands for Confidentiality, Integrity, and Availability. Which best describes the integrity of data?
    A. A lack of viruses
    B. Senior manager level access only
    C. When the encrypted data is the same size as the data before encryption
    D. The level to which the data approximates the truth

18. Sometimes organizations decide to keep the personal data collected for a longer period than initially predicted. What is not a consequence of an increased data retention period?
    A. An increase in data availability
    B. The need for the collection purpose to cover the increase in retention
    C. A reduction in the risk of a data breach
    D. The longer retention period does not necessarily affect the data integrity

19. Organizations value personal data, and when they see another purpose for it, they are inclined to re-use the personal data. Which principle prevents an organization from re-using personal data limitlessly?
   A. Lawful processing criteria
   B. Purpose limitation
   C. Data integrity
   D. Data availability

20. For which of the following activities is there no exception for processing sensitive personal data in the GDPR?
   A. Financial data processing
   B. Journalism
   C. Scientific research
   D. Human resources

This information can be used for the following four questions:

You are the manager of a Los Angeles-based tailor for plus-sized clothing. The specialization of your company is to take popular designs and adapt them to the size and shape of the customer.

Your customers are from all over the world. In order to create the clothing, customers measure specific points of their body, allowing the tailor to get an idea of the customer's needs. The customers fill out an order form with these measurements and choose the design they want to order. The tailor then creates the suit, dress or shoes, and ships the order to the customer.

Recently, the tailor opened a workshop in Milan to supply the European market. However, the workshop in Milan does not have the capacity to create all designs in the catalog, and certain items still come from the Los Angeles workshop.

21. To explore the market, the tailor uses a social media tracking pixel on its website. For its European visitors, what is most likely required?
    A. A notice that indicates it concerns a third-party pixel and the user should use an add-blocker if they do not wish to be tracked
    B. A cookie notice
    C. Block access to the website until a user agrees
    D. Consent before placing the tracking pixel

22. The retailer provides a portal for customers to upload the information needed to create the clothes. What is this platform most likely?
    A. Cloud computing
    B. Multi-factor authentication
    C. Social networking
    D. Direct marketing

23. The retailer shares personal data between both workshops. Which of the following is not a mechanism that would allow this?
    A. Standard contractual clauses
    B. Binding corporate rules
    C. A data processing agreement
    D. A replacement of privacy shield

24. A data subject from the EU claims that the information about her size and shape she provided is sensitive personal data and would like the personal data to be deleted. Which of the following is most appropriate?
    A. The personal data in Los Angeles needs to be deleted
    B. Only the personal data kept in Europe needs to be deleted
    C. The personal data was supplied in order to perform a contract, so it does not need to be deleted
    D. The GDPR does not apply, since the tailor is headquartered in Los Angeles

25. How can the lawful processing criterion from Article 6f best be described?
    A. A balancing of the interests of the controller and the data subject
    B. A reason for objecting against the processing
    C. A definite justification for the processing of personal data
    D. A claim the data subject communicates to the processor after he/she becomes aware of the processing

26. For which processing would the lawful processing criterion legitimate interest most likely apply?
    A. Job interview preparation
    B. Shipping a customer's order
    C. The European Commission processing any personal data
    D. Digital marketing e-mails with an opt-out possibility

27. When using the lawful processing criterion performance of a contract, what is a necessity?
    A. The contract must be notarized
    B. The data subject must be a party to the contract
    C. There must be two parties to the contract
    D. The contract must be in writing

28. What is true for the lawful processing criteria and sensitive personal data?
    A. Any sensitive personal data willingly provided is to be considered manifestly made public
    B. Leaked personal data can no longer be considered sensitive
    C. Journalists can process any sensitive personal data
    D. Unless an exception applies, consent is required

29. Which of the following does not describe the correct timing of a privacy notice?
    A. A privacy notice, which goes beyond explaining the use of cookies, presented directly when opening a website
    B. A privacy notice when you are requested to enable the Bluetooth functionality of your phone
    C. A sign indicating the use of CCTV, including some additional information, at the moment of entering the area where the CCTV is in use
    D. Together with the advertisement e-mail for an organization's mailing list

30. Your organization performs several types of processing, and several types of data subjects are involved. The privacy notice has become very long. What is the most appropriate solution?
    A. Use a layered privacy notice
    B. Let the data protection authority approve the privacy notice
    C. Make sure all the legal terms are in the notice
    D. Make the notice available in writing

31. Which of the following likely complies least with the transparency principle?
    A. Listing the incorrect lawful processing criterion in the privacy notice
    B. Using the personal data in an undisclosed second process
    C. Not disclosing the processing to the data protection authority
    D. Refusing to meet with the data protection authority at a certain time

32. Many websites contain a privacy notice. Which of the following best describes a privacy notice?
    A. A list of mandatory information to be disclosed to the data subject
    B. Information to be provided to the data protection authority
    C. A contract between the data subject and the controller
    D. A contract between the data subject and the processor

33. At which point is a website required to make its privacy notice available?
    A. Before placing any cookies that can lead to the identification of the visitor
    B. Before placing functional cookies on a visitor's device
    C. Before analytical cookies are downloaded
    D. Before placing tracking cookies

34. If you are a citizen of the US, and your personal data is processed by a retail organization in the EU, which of the following is most likely not applicable?
    A. You have the right to object to the processing
    B. Binding Corporate Rules do not need to be in place
    C. You have the right to have your personal data corrected
    D. You have the right to be informed prior to the processing

35. Organizations are required to inform data subjects if the processing involves automated decision-making. Which of the following best describes automated decision-making?
   A. The use of quantum computing
   B. The review of CVs by the HR department
   C. Criteria for selection programmed in by someone involved in the selection process
   D. Use of audit software that automatically performs certain tests

36. Consent is one of the legal processing criteria that can be relied on. Which are the criteria for consent provided by a data subject?
   A. Reversible, written, machine-readable
   B. Provided by the parents of the data subject
   C. Explicit, freely given, specific
   D. A written and signed form with the date of consent

37. A data subject's request for erasure is not always honored. What could be a valid reason for refusal?
   A. There is a lawful processing criterion that prevents deletion of the personal data
   B. The amount of work it is for the controller can outweigh the data subject's right in most cases
   C. If the data subject has provided consent, the controller does not need to delete the personal data
   D. If the contract has been fulfilled, but the controller has an internal policy to keep the personal data for longer

38. What is a possible privacy risk when combining several unrevealing data elements about someone?
   A. Unintentionally decrypting personal data
   B. Accidentally decompressing personal data
   C. The data can become corrupted
   D. The combining can result in profiling

39. An organization receives a request from a data subject to see all personal data the organization processes on him/her. Which of the following is most applicable?
    A. The request can be put on hold if the organization has financial issues
    B. Only unencrypted data needs to be provided
    C. The organization has to verify in its processes whether it processes any personal data on that person
    D. A data subject can oblige the organization to provide the personal data on a USB stick, so it is machine-readable

40. How can the term "appropriate technical and organizational measures" best be described?
    A. A level of file protection appropriate for the risk
    B. Installing malware scanners for all computers, including those not connected to the internet
    C. Applying role-based access control, restricting every file to access by the CEO only
    D. A level of measures to protect the data appropriate for the risk

41. Based on what is a controller most likely allowed to audit the processor it uses?
    A. The GDPR
    B. A data protection authority notice
    C. The data processing agreement
    D. The controller's authority

42. For large files that may cause an organization to run out of space, what would be an appropriate technical measure to prevent a data breach?
    A. Deleting files
    B. Removal of metadata
    C. Role-based access control
    D. Compression

43. For an organization with frequent staff changes, what would be an appropriate organizational measure to prevent a data breach?
    A. Complicated password requirements
    B. Appoint the role of the security officer to the data protection officer
    C. Require the staff to bring its own device
    D. Role-based access control

44. A data processing agreement can be required before starting to process personal data. Which best describes a data processing agreement?
    A. An agreement the processor is obliged to let the controller sign before the controller starts processing personal data
    B. An agreement between the controller and processor detailing the level of security, as well as other details regarding the processing
    C. An agreement that makes agreements with sub-processors obsolete
    D. A document describing how data is processed in the different affiliates of a multi-national organization

45. Which most incorrectly describes a data processing impact assessment?
    A. A balancing of interests of the controller versus the data subjects
    B. A risk assessment
    C. An inventory of mitigated and unmitigated risks
    D. A (sometimes) mandatory assessment

46. The data protection officer has a special position in an organization. How can the position/role/job of the data protection officer not be described?
    A. Independent
    B. Working in the interest of the shareholder
    C. Reporting to the highest level of management
    D. Providing the data protection authority with information

47. A data protection officer can be mandatory for an organization to appoint. In which case is it most likely that an organization needs to appoint a data protection officer?
    A. An average organization
    B. A US-based retailer
    C. A government-funded university
    D. A chemical research facility with over 250 staff members

48. What is the likely course of action after a data protection impact assessment has shown that some risks cannot be brought down to an acceptable level?
    A. Continue the processing regardless, as you have done all you can
    B. Inform the Data Protection Authority
    C. Inform the data subjects of the data breach
    D. Reserve budget for a fine

49. Many organizations maintain a data processing inventory. What is the biggest benefit of performing a data processing inventory?
    A. Being able to quickly see any processing that shares data elements with other processing
    B. Being compliant with the GDPR
    C. Knowing where to direct the attention of the chief information security officer
    D. Being able to determine whether it is required to appoint a data protection officer

50. When a data subject complains to the data protection authority, the data protection authority can start an investigation. What is the most likely role of the organization's data protection officer in this case?
    A. Send the data protection authority the data on all the organization's employees
    B. The data protection officer is part of the investigation team
    C. Act as the point of contact for the data protection authority
    D. The data protection officer approves all the communication between the organization and the data protection authority

51. The Human Resources department of a company processes (sensitive) personal data. What is likely not appropriate processing of personal data?
    A. Receiving information from the company doctor about employees
    B. Using photographs of staff on the company website
    C. Process the sensitive personal data for social security purposes
    D. Process the sensitive personal data for wage payment purpose

52. What is the issue/problem with asking employees for consent as an employer?
    A. The employer pays the employee
    B. Consent at work cannot be registered in the employee's file
    C. The employees likely feel pressure to provide consent
    D. There are limits to what consent can be asked for

This information can be used for the following four questions:

Due to a recent crisis, all education takes place online. In order to attend classes, students log on to a free video call service. The teacher then shares the lesson materials on the screen through the video call service and talks the students through the lesson.

Attendance is not monitored, because some parents objected to the processing. The school, scared by the parents and feeling pressured to accommodate for the sake of the students, decided students do not need to take part in the class live. Those students are allowed to download the recording of the class later.

53. In order to record the class, the school asks for the teachers' permission. What can be a difficulty in asking the teachers for permission?
   A. It will be impossible to get consent in writing
   B. Once the consent for the recordings is obtained, it cannot be withdrawn
   C. The school is the teachers' employer, and the teachers might feel pressured
   D. No possible other legal processing criterion is applicable

54. If the students are willfully recorded by the school without disclosing it to the students or parents, and a data breach takes place resulting in the spread of a video of one of the students picking his nose, what is a possible scenario?
   A. The data protection authority forces the school to perform a data protection impact assessment to correct the breach
   B. A claim based on Article 82
   C. Forced closure of the school
   D. Retroactive consent of the parents, rectifying the situation

55. Which of the following is not necessarily required before starting to process personal data in order to provide classes online?
    A. A lawful processing criterion
    B. A data protection impact assessment
    C. A privacy notice
    D. Consent

56. What would be an example of the proportionality principle in this case?
    A. Requiring parents to consent
    B. Performing a data protection impact assessment
    C. Requiring the use of software for which a data processing agreement is in place
    D. Not requiring students to turn on their camera

57. Software can be installed that monitors the amount of data that leaves the network and intervenes when this seems excessive. What is this called?
    A. Leak fixing
    B. A policy control
    C. Data Loss Prevention
    D. Data breach reporting

58. Which body/institution/organization do the directorates-general (departments) of the European Commission report with regards to data protection?
    A. The European Data Protection Supervisor
    B. The European Data Protection Board
    C. The Data Protection Agency in the country where the directorate-general is located
    D. The European Data Protection Authority

59. Of the following, which is the least fitting description of the European Data Protection Board?
    A. The authority that supervises the national data protection authorities
    B. The new version of the Working Party 29
    C. A collection of representatives of national data protection authorities
    D. An organization headquartered in Brussels

60. An organization delivers folders to a certain neighborhood. Which of the following is required?
    A. Legitimate interest
    B. Respecting "no unaddressed mail" stickers
    C. An opt-out opportunity
    D. An opt-in opportunity

61. Tracking technologies can help identify visitors that have also visited certain other websites. Which of the following is possibly a tracking technology?
    A. Analytical cookies
    B. Web beacons
    C. Functional cookies
    D. An HTTPS connection

62. Personal use of personal data falls outside the scope of the General Data Protection regulation. Which of the following is most likely personal use of personal data?
    A. The use by a user of a social network website of family information
    B. The scraping of Twitter for scientific research
    C. A doctor giving a patient test results
    D. A company analyzing DNA at the request of individuals

63. The data protection authority can investigate an organization. Which of the following is not a possible role of the data protection officer when the data protection authority is conducting an investigation?
    A. Being a contact person for the data protection authority
    B. Representing the organization
    C. Informing the CEO of the organization of the practices of the organization
    D. Performing data protection impact assessments to assess the situation

64. Artificial Intelligence can be taught (or learn) to create datasets from publicly available information. Which of the following is the most likely privacy risk?
    A. Artificial Intelligence can use your personal data against you
    B. At a certain point, Artificial Intelligence will get out of control
    C. Artificial intelligence will not be able to determine whether something is personal data
    D. Newly generated data sets reveal new personal data

This information can be used for the following four questions:

An international taxi company drives between Hungary, Serbia, and Croatia. The company has offices in all three countries, but the head office is located in Serbia.

The company focuses on business customers and mostly drives around clients within one of the three countries. However, international trips do occur, and the national offices communicate data of both drivers and customers with the head office.

At a certain point, an employee at the head office opens an attachment that asks the employee to log in with his company username and password. The employee didn't recognize this was a phishing attack and entered the information.

The party behind the phishing e-mail then used the employee's credentials to log on to the network of the taxi company.

65. After discovering what happened with the phishing e-mail, what should be the company's course of action?
    A. Report the breach to the data protection authority in Serbia
    B. Report the breach to the European Data Protection Supervisor
    C. Assess the situation and determine what exactly has been accessed
    D. Investigate and report to the relevant data protection authority after the investigation has finished

66. To share the employee data and customer data with other branches, which of the following is required to allow the exchange?
    A. Privacy shield
    B. Data processing agreement
    C. Binding corporate rules
    D. A data protection impact assessment

67. Which would have the most impact on preventing the success of the phishing attack?
    A. Multi-factor authentication
    B. Scanning for viruses
    C. Scanning for malware
    D. Complicated passwords

68. The drivers use an application on their private phones to communicate regarding customers and use the navigation system to the destination. What is most recommended for the company to have in place for this specific situation?
    A. Opt-out possibilities for the driver
    B. Ensuring the use of the application is for the benefit of the driver
    C. Forcing the drivers to opt-in to the use of the application
    D. A bring your own device program

69. New technologies can result in unforeseen privacy risks. Which of the following is the least likely to result in unforeseen privacy risks?
    A. Geolocation
    B. Biometric identification
    C. Mainframe storage
    D. CCTV

70. Before changing an aspect of work that could impact privacy, works councils are often asked for input. Which of the following is most likely a task of the works councils?
    A. Provide positive or negative advice
    B. To approve a strike
    C. Decide on which route to take
    D. Perform a data protection impact assessment

71. Geolocation data can reveal where a device is at a certain time. When is geolocation most likely going to lead to processing personal data?
    A. When an organization keeps track of its cars
    B. When every device has a geolocation checker with no ID
    C. If geolocation is only active when a device is lost
    D. When a GPS device is used independently of vehicles

72. In the US, the GDPR does not necessarily apply to direct marketing. Which law most likely applies to direct marketing in the US?
    A. CAN-SPAM
    B. POPI Act
    C. The e-privacy directive
    D. PIPEDA

73. When is marketing by regular mail least likely covered by the GDPR or e-privacy directive?
    A. When the mail is sent to the US
    B. When the mail is sent from an adequate country
    C. When the mail is sent unaddressed
    D. In case a prior business relationship exists

74. The GDPR can be difficult to interpret, and organizations often require guidance. Where would the interpretation of the GDPR likely be discussed amongst data protection authorities?
    A. The investigations of the data protection authority
    B. The data protection authority conference
    C. The data protection officer meeting
    D. At meetings of the European Data Protection Board

75. What can be a reason to refuse a data portability request?
    A. There is a legitimate processing criterion in place
    B. A two-time extension has passed
    C. The controller refuses a valid form of identification in preference of another form of identification
    D. The data was not provided by the data subject

76. Data is often collected without realizing that it concerns biometric data. Which of the following is least likely going to result in the collection of biometric data?
    A. A speed camera focused on the front of the car
    B. A chip in an identification card
    C. A temperature check at the entrance of an office building
    D. CCTV camera use

77. The right to be forgotten can be used to force an organization to delete a data subject's personal data under certain conditions. Which of the following is an important consideration for an organization when receiving a request like that?
    A. Ensuring backups are taken into account
    B. Creating a barrier as high as possible
    C. Figuring out a new purpose and new lawful processing criterion to keep processing the data
    D. Requesting a fee for the deletion due to the amount of work

78. Canada is considered partially adequate. Which part of Canada is considered adequate?
    A. The government institutions
    B. The entire country, covered by Safe Harbor
    C. The French part of Canada
    D. The part covered by the Personal Information Protection and Electronic Documents Act

79. An organization does not always process personal data itself. What kind of entities can ask other organizations to perform processing for them?
   A. Controllers
   B. Controllers or processors
   C. Sub-processors
   D. Organizations with an adequacy decision

80. Organizations don't keep their data forever. What is a schedule on when to delete data also referred to as?
   A. A data retention scheme
   B. A data deletion policy
   C. A data policy
   D. A formatting scheme

81. When creating a data retention scheme, what is the least important consideration?
   A. Whether the cloud server is of sufficient size
   B. For which period the lawful processing criterion is applicable
   C. At which point the collection purpose has been achieved
   D. Which processes use the personal data

82. Organizations outside the EU can process personal data on citizens of the EU. In which of the following situations does the GDPR most likely apply?
   A. An Argentinian football club's international fan club
   B. An American web shop
   C. A Canadian web shop
   D. The South African army

83. Before processing personal data, the data subject has the right to be informed. Which of the following is not part of the information the controller is obliged to provide?
    A. The exact data storage location
    B. The retention period
    C. The lawful processing criterion
    D. The purpose for which the data is collected

84. Organizations can create a set of binding corporate rules for international data transfers. What is not an aspect/property of binding corporate rules?
    A. It applies to both the EU and non-EU affiliates
    B. Standard contractual clauses are no longer required
    C. No deviations from the GDPR are included
    D. A copy of the data processing inventory is included

85. Certain measures are not necessary if a country is considered adequate. Which institution/organization/body issues adequacy decisions?
    A. The European Parliament
    B. The European Data Protection Supervisor
    C. The European Data Protection Board
    D. The European Commission

This information can be used for the following three questions:

A real estate company that rents out apartments maintains an elaborate database of its tenants. The company owns many large apartment buildings, both in Romania and Hungary.

The tenants are citizens from all walks of life, and the real estate company stores the financial history of the tenant, indicating whether there have been payment issues in the past. Only the history of payments to the real estate agency is used to judge the tenants' financial reliability.

Naturally, the company processes large quantities of personal data. This is necessary for sending the right bill to the right tenant and arranging the necessary maintenance.

86. When potential tenants send their interest for a certain apartment, there is a box to tick in case they do not want to receive e-mails informing them of vacant apartments. What is this called?
    A. Opt-in
    B. Explicit consent for further processing
    C. Opt-out
    D. Irreversible

87. When the company sends e-mails to persons that did not tick the box not to receive further e-mails, what is the likely lawful processing criterion?
    A. Performance of a contract
    B. Consent
    C. Legitimate interest
    D. Vital interest

88. The agency uses CCTV in its buildings to protect the safety of the tenants. What is an important consideration in this case?
    A. Ensuring the cameras are not revealing the inside of the apartments
    B. Ensuring no activity in the elevator is revealed
    C. Ensuring all tenants are provided with the opportunity to opt-out
    D. Ensuring no children are filmed

89. Social media organizations are known for providing tracking pixels. What is a use of these tracking pixels?
    A. Targeted advertisement
    B. Informing data subjects
    C. Linking of website to website
    D. Masking IP addresses

90. What can most likely be a complicated privacy issue with whistleblower policies?
    A. Protecting one identity can increase the likelihood of unjust harm to the other
    B. There is no encryption sufficiently strong to be considered adequate
    C. Works council involvement
    D. The bureaucracy that follows can lead to mandatory disclosure of identity

Answer key exam 1:
1A, 2D, 3C, 4D, 5A, 6B, 7C, 8C, 9A, 10B, 11D, 12A, 13C, 14B,
15B, 16B, 17D, 18C, 19B, 20A, 21D, 22A, 23C, 24A, 25A, 26D,
27B, 28D, 29D, 30A, 31B, 32A, 33A, 34A, 35C, 36C, 37A, 38D,
39C, 40D, 41C, 42D, 43D, 44B, 45A, 46B, 47C, 48B, 49A, 50C,
51B, 52C, 53C, 54B, 55D, 56D, 57C, 58A, 59A, 60B, 61B, 62A,
63B, 64D, 65C, 66C, 67A, 68D, 69C, 70A, 71A, 72A, 73C, 74D,
75D, 76B, 77A, 78D, 79B, 80A, 81A, 82A, 83A, 84D, 85D, 86C,
87C, 88A, 89A, 90A

Correct answers and explanations for exam 1:

1. Several treaties have played an important part in the establishment of the European Union. Which two treaties did the Treaty of Lisbon amend?
   A. The Treaty of Maastricht and the Treaty of Rome (correct)
   B. The Treaty of Amsterdam and the Treaty of Madrid
   C. The Treaty of Paris and the Geneva Convention
   D. Directive 95 and the E-Privacy Directive

Info:

A is the correct answer. The Treaty of Maastricht and the Treaty of Rome are the two treaties you will need to remember, as well as the Treaty of Lisbon, which amended these treaties.

2. The European Union consists of several institutions and agencies. Which of the following institutions is least involved in the drafting, approval, or monitoring of the GDPR?
   A. The European Data Protection Board
   B. The European Parliament
   C. The European Commission
   D. The European Data Protection Supervisor (correct)

Info:

D is the correct answer. The EDPS does nothing with the GDPR but is the organization that supervises the use of personal data in the EU Institutions, which fall under a different data protection regulation (Regulation 2018/1725).

3. Several courts are accessible at both a national and an international level. Which court has the final say if a case is taken to a higher court the maximum number of times?
   A. The National Court
   B. The European Data Protection Court
   C. The European Court of Justice (correct)
   D. The European Data Protection Board

Info:
C is the correct answer. National courts can refer the case to the European Court of Justice. Sometimes national cases can appeal to the European Court of Justice, if it pertains to European law (such as data protection law).

4. Before the GDPR, there was Directive 95(the Data Protection Directive). Which is the most impactful difference between the GDPR and Directive 95?
   A. The GDPR adequately describes data subjects
   B. Data subjects have gotten the right to access their personal data under the GDPR
   C. Article 82 of the GDPR allows for data protection authorities to issue fines
   D. The GDPR is a Regulation, and the Directive 95 is a Directive (correct)

Info:
D is the correct answer. The thing to remember here is that a regulation provides less freedom for the Member States on how to implement the articles of the regulation. A directive leaves more freedom, and therefore the Member States had differing ways/levels of data protection before the GDPR.

5. Laws in the EU go through a lengthy process, both for its development and approval. Which two EU institutions vote on a law?

   A. The EU Parliament and the Council (correct)
   B. The European Court of Auditors and the European Commission
   C. The European Commission and the European Court of Justice
   D. The European Court of Justice and the Council

Info:

A is the correct answer. The European Parliament and the Council of the European Union (the Council) are the institutions that have an actual vote. The European Commission is mostly involved in the drafting, and the European Court of Justice is involved in the interpretation. The Court of Auditors is not involved.

6. Some more laws and regulations pertain to privacy and data protection, it is not just the GDPR. Which legislation is also referred to as the cookie directive?

   A. The GDPR
   B. An amendment to the e-privacy directive (correct)
   C. CAN-SPAM
   D. Directive 95

Info:

B is the correct answer. The e-privacy directive addresses privacy and electronic communication, and one of its amendments is also referred to as the cookie directive. Keep in mind that this pertains to electronic communication, so, for example, it does not apply to regular mail.

7. Which of the following is most likely covered by the EU Directive on privacy and electronic communications?
   A. Snail mail marketing
   B. An internet provider's HR records
   C. **A retailer's marketing e-mails (correct)**
   D. Recovery of unencrypted hard drives

Info:
C is the correct answer. Of the options provided, marketing e-mail is the only option that fits the scope of the e-privacy directive, since it is electronic (mail) communication.

8. Personal data can be described as anything that says something about anyone. Which of the following options best fits the definition of personal data?
   A. A single GPS location
   B. A copy of a deleted e-mail with the address removed
   C. **The nickname someone uses online, and the data attached to it (correct)**
   D. Anonymized data about someone's online activity

Info:
C is the correct answer. A nickname alone likely does not say anything about a natural person (unless it contains references that allow identification), but the data connected to a nickname can quite likely lead to identification. Think of the same nickname being used on different websites as well, and how revealing it can be if all the actions under that nickname are linked.

9. A controller can be an organization that determines the means and purposes of the processing of personal data. Which of the following activities best fits the definition of a controller?

   A. A restaurant only accepts reservations by phone and doesn't use a computerized reservation system (correct)

   B. An organization performs data analytics on datasets provided by your organization

   C. A cloud storage provider that offers a certain level of security

   D. A delivery company that processes the list of delivery locations for its corporate customers

Info:

A is the correct answer. The restaurant is in full control of the personal data (reservations). The other options describe organizations that are instructed by others (processors).

10. Not all data should be considered personal data. In which instance is the data most likely not considered personal data?

    A. A series of bank account transactions, with the bank account number and name removed

    B. A dataset processed by a processor, which is not covered by the Data Processing Agreement (correct)

    C. A copy of a dataset, with the names not visible on the copy

    D. Publicly available data about someone, not of a sensitive nature

Info:

B is the correct answer. If the data is personal data, it should be covered by the data processing agreement. Since option B describes data that is not covered by a data processing agreement, this means it is likely not personal data (assuming that the controller did not make a mistake, of course). All other options can (theoretically) lead to identification.

11. It may not always be clear whether a certain way of processing reveals sensitive personal data. Which of the following most likely reveals sensitive personal data?
    A. Someone's bank account balance
    B. A public computer's browsing history
    C. A corrupted hard drive that previously contained sensitive data about someone
    D. A nationality in a passport (correct)

Info:

D is the correct answer. Certain countries, for example, claim that their nationals are only of a certain religion. For that reason, if a person has that nationality, you need to take into account the likeliness of that person being of a certain religion. Religion, of course, is sensitive personal data. To be clear, a nationality itself is not sensitive personal data, but it can reveal sensitive personal data. This can be difficult to understand, but keep this rule in mind when you encounter a question like this.

12. Open text fields are often used at the end of a survey for information that didn't fit in multiple-choice form. When using an open text field in a company survey, what is a possible negative consequence?
    A. A respondent possibly (mis)uses it to enter sensitive personal data (correct)
    B. Consent is required for the processing of the survey
    C. The retention period of the survey will need to be further restricted
    D. A Data Protection Impact Assessment is required

Info:

A is the correct answer. An open text field is a box where you can enter whatever you want (instead of selecting an answer or following a certain format such as a date). Since you can write whatever you want in an open text field, this means you can also write sensitive personal data.

13. Not every process contains personal data. Which of the following is not necessarily considered processing of personal data?
    A. Storing employee self-assessments
    B. Sending paychecks to personal addresses
    C. Requesting someone to provide his/her medical records (correct)
    D. Transferring financial data to the tax authorities

Info:

C is the correct answer. This might be formulated misleadingly since medical records are personal data. However, the request itself is not processing yet. It could be the case if it is a targeted request for example, but that is not mentioned so from the options provided C is the best choice.

14. The GDPR can be applicable in cases you don't expect, especially with the global way of doing business nowadays. To which of the following does the GDPR least likely apply?
    A. A German producer of consumer goods
    B. A non-EU producer selling globally through a local reseller (correct)
    C. A Swedish meatball restaurant
    D. A French organization, focusing on data analytics in the US

Info:

B is the correct answer. Of the options provided, this is the only option where the GDPR does not apply necessarily. It could be the case that the local reseller orders without providing personal data of the final customers, and then resells. To the reseller, the GDPR then applies (if selling in the EU), but not to the producer.

15. If you are an Australian citizen, when does the GDPR provide protection for the use of your personal data?
    A. When abroad, outside of the EU
    B. **When ordering from a German-based global retailer (correct)**
    C. When working for an Australian company that mainly deals with EU businesses
    D. Hardly ever, Australia is not part of the EU nor does Australia have a treaty with the EU regarding data protection

Info:

B is the correct answer. Even personal data of non-EU citizens is protected under the GDPR when processed in the EU. In this case, the retailer is based in Germany, and therefore the personal data is (likely) processed in Germany.

16. Processing personal data under the GDPR requires a lawful processing criterion to be applicable. Which lawful processing criterion would you use as a retailer to process someone's name & address for shipping the ordered item?
    A. Consent
    B. **Necessary for the performance of a contract (correct)**
    C. Protection of vital interest of the data subject
    D. Necessary for the performance of a public task

Info:

B is the correct answer. This can be seen as a purchase contract, and of course the retailer will need to process personal data of the customer (name, address) to complete the purchase contract. This does not mean the personal data can be stored longer than necessary, so once the contract is completed the personal data needs to be deleted.

17. CIA stands for Confidentiality, Integrity, and Availability. Which best describes the integrity of data?
    A. A lack of viruses
    B. Senior manager level access only
    C. When the encrypted data is the same size as the data before encryption
    D. The level to which the data approximates the truth (correct)

Info:

D is the correct answer. Integrity refers to the data not being impaired, therefore, assuming that the original data contains data that is true, D is the correct answer. If, for example, a hacker has altered the data of an organization (thus it is not reflecting the original/true data anymore), the integrity of the data is affected.

18. Sometimes organizations decide to keep the personal data collected for a longer period than initially predicted. What is not a consequence of an increased data retention period?
    A. An increase in data availability
    B. The need for the collection purpose to cover the increase in retention
    C. A reduction in the risk of a data breach (correct)
    D. The longer retention period does not necessarily affect the data integrity

Info:

C is the correct answer. When you keep personal data for a longer period, there is more time in which a data breach can occur, therefore increasing the risk. Think of doing something dangerous for a longer time, this will increase the likeliness of something going wrong, and one definition of risk is "likeliness x adverse consequence".

19. Organizations value personal data, and when they see another purpose for it, they are inclined to re-use the personal data. Which principle prevents an organization from re-using personal data limitlessly?
    A. Lawful processing criteria
    B. Purpose limitation (correct)
    C. Data integrity
    D. Data availability

Info:

B is the correct answer. If you collect the personal data for one purpose, you can't use it for another purpose (unless you find a new lawful processing criterion). This is referred to as purpose limitation.

20. For which of the following activities is there no exception for processing sensitive personal data in the GDPR?
    A. Financial data processing (correct)
    B. Journalism
    C. Scientific research
    D. Human resources

Info:

A is the correct answer. Article 9 of the GDPR does not apply to financial data processing (whatever that is). You can also guess this answer by thinking of the likely reasoning behind the restriction. For B, C, and D it is obvious that completely forbidding the processing of sensitive personal data will significantly impair the possibilities (and thus negatively impact the quality of science and journalism). For human resources, there are revealing elements, such as gender and whether someone is married, that need to be processed.

This information can be used for the following four questions:

You are the manager of a Los Angeles-based tailor for plus-sized clothing. The specialization of your company is to take popular designs and adapt them to the size and shape of the customer.

Your customers are from all over the world. In order to create the clothing, customers measure specific points of their body, allowing the tailor to get an idea of the customer's needs. The customers fill out an order form with these measurements and choose the design they want to order. The tailor then creates the suit, dress or shoes, and ships the order to the customer.

Recently, the tailor opened a workshop in Milan to supply the European market. However, the workshop in Milan does not have the capacity to create all designs in the catalog, and certain items still come from the Los Angeles workshop.

21. To explore the market, the tailor uses a social media tracking pixel on its website. For its European visitors, what is most likely required?
    A. A notice that indicates it concerns a third-party pixel and the user should use an add-blocker if they do not wish to be tracked
    B. A cookie notice
    C. Block access to the website until a user agrees
    D. **Consent before placing the tracking pixel (correct)**

Info:

D is the correct answer. The tracking pixel (also called a web beacon) will likely send data about the visitor to the social media website. The social media website will register the device's IP address and that it visited the website (perhaps even at a certain time), and will try to link it to the profile of the user(s) that also use the social media website with that IP address. There is no likely reason for this that would be relevant for the functioning of the website, and therefore consent is likely needed for this practice.

22. The retailer provides a portal for customers to upload the information needed to create the clothes. What is this platform most likely?
    A. **Cloud computing (correct)**
    B. Multi-factor authentication
    C. Social networking
    D. Direct marketing

Info:

A is the correct answer. The data is likely stored on a network, and a simple definition of cloud computing is processing data on a network.

23. The retailer shares personal data between both workshops. Which of the following is not a mechanism that would allow this?
    A. Standard contractual clauses
    B. Binding corporate rules
    C. **A data processing agreement (correct)**
    D. A replacement of privacy shield

Info:

C is the correct answer. If the organization shares the data internally, this is still the same organization (and the controller). A data processing agreement would only be required if data were processed by a third/external party under the control of the controller (a processor).

24. A data subject from the EU claims that the information about her size and shape she provided is sensitive personal data and would like the personal data to be deleted. Which of the following is most appropriate?
   A. **The personal data in Los Angeles needs to be deleted (correct)**
   B. Only the personal data kept in Europe needs to be deleted
   C. The personal data was supplied in order to perform a contract, so it does not need to be deleted
   D. The GDPR does not apply, since the tailor is headquartered in Los Angeles

Info:

A is the correct answer. For this organization, it is safe to assume that they target EU citizens as well given the workshop in Milan. When EU citizens are targeted, the GDPR applies, including the right to have your personal data deleted (with some exceptions). This applies to both sensitive and non-sensitive personal data, so the part about being sensitive is not relevant here.

25. How can the lawful processing criterion from Article 6f best be described?
   A. **A balancing of the interests of the controller and the data subject (correct)**
   B. A reason for objecting against the processing
   C. A definite justification for the processing of personal data
   D. A claim the data subject communicates to the processor after he/she becomes aware of the processing

Info:

A is the correct answer. Article 6f, or often referred to as "legitimate interest", requires a balancing of the interest of the controller and the data subject. If the conclusion is that, for example, the impact on the person's privacy is insignificant and the interests of the controller outweigh the privacy of the data subject, then this lawful processing criterion can be relied on.

26. For which processing would the lawful processing criterion legitimate interest most likely apply?
   A. Job interview preparation
   B. Shipping a customer's order
   C. The European Commission processing any personal data
   D. Digital marketing e-mails with an opt-out possibility (correct)

Info:

D is the correct answer. The first two options are likely done under "necessary for the performance of a contract", and the European Commission does not fall under the GDPR for a lot of its processing of personal data (and in addition, the legislation applicable to the European Commission does not allow processing based on "legitimate interest"). So that leaves D, and especially the part that there is an opt-out possibility gives away that it is based on "legitimate interest".

27. When using the lawful processing criterion performance of a contract, what is a necessity?
   A. The contract must be notarized
   B. The data subject must be a party to the contract (correct)
   C. There must be two parties to the contract
   D. The contract must be in writing

Info:

B is the correct answer. You cannot simply process someone's personal data for the performance of a contract if it is for a contract with someone else. If a controller has a contract with you, it cannot process my personal data using the lawful processing criterion "performance of a contract".

28. What is true for the lawful processing criteria and sensitive personal data?
    A. Any sensitive personal data willingly provided is to be considered manifestly made public
    B. Leaked personal data can no longer be considered sensitive
    C. Journalists can process any sensitive personal data
    D. Unless an exception applies, consent is required (correct)

Info:

D is the correct answer. There are a few exceptions, as you saw with earlier questions, but generally, consent is required to process sensitive personal data.

29. Which of the following does not describe the correct timing of a privacy notice?
    A. A privacy notice, which goes beyond explaining the use of cookies, presented directly when opening a website
    B. A privacy notice when you are requested to enable the Bluetooth functionality of your phone
    C. A sign indicating the use of CCTV, including some additional information, at the moment of entering the area where the CCTV is in use
    D. Together with the advertisement e-mail for an organization's mailing list (correct)

Info:

D is the correct answer. The privacy notice should be provided <u>before</u> the processing of personal data starts (unless an exception applies). Here, it was quite possible to provide the privacy notice before sending out the e-mail, for example when collecting the e-mail address.

30. Your organization performs several types of processing, and several types of data subjects are involved. The privacy notice has become very long. What is the most appropriate solution?
   A. **Use a layered privacy notice (correct)**
   B. Let the data protection authority approve the privacy notice
   C. Make sure all the legal terms are in the notice
   D. Make the notice available in writing

Info:

A is the correct answer. A privacy notice needs to be readable, which is getting harder if the privacy notice gets too long. A possible solution here would be to present only the relevant information, and a layered privacy notice allows for this since only the information for the part the user clicks on is presented. Therefore, only the information for the types of processing the user wants to read is presented at once, making it more readable.

31. Which of the following likely complies least with the transparency principle?
   A. Listing the incorrect lawful processing criterion in the privacy notice
   B. **Using the personal data in an undisclosed second process (correct)**
   C. Not disclosing the processing to the data protection authority
   D. Refusing to meet with the data protection authority at a certain time

Info:

B is the correct answer. Not disclosing the processing violates the transparency principle. The processing needs to be explained in a privacy notice before starting the processing, and if you start a second sort of processing, this also needs to be disclosed. If you rely on consent, the consent needs to be updated as well.

32. Many websites contain a privacy notice. Which of the following best describes a privacy notice?
   A. **A list of mandatory information to be disclosed to the data subject (correct)**
   B. Information to be provided to the data protection authority
   C. A contract between the data subject and the controller
   D. A contract between the data subject and the processor

Info:

A is the correct answer. Article 12 and 13 of the GDPR are clear on the information that needs to be provided, and the document in which this information is provided is generally referred to as a privacy notice.

33. At which point is a website required to make its privacy notice available?
   A. **Before placing any cookies that can lead to the identification of the visitor (correct)**
   B. Before placing functional cookies on a visitor's device
   C. Before analytical cookies are downloaded
   D. Before placing tracking cookies

Info:

A is the correct answer. Placing a cookie (such as analytical or tracking) can lead to the processing of personal data. Since a privacy notice needs to be provided before the processing of personal data, the privacy notice needs to be provided before placing cookies that result in processing personal data. Options C and D could possibly lead to the identification of the data subject, but the answers are incomplete.

34. If you are a citizen of the US, and your personal data is processed by a retail organization in the EU, which of the following is most likely not applicable?
   A. **You have the right to object to the processing (correct)**
   B. Binding Corporate Rules do not need to be in place
   C. You have the right to have your personal data corrected
   D. You have the right to be informed prior to the processing

Info:

A is the correct answer. Having the right to object to the processing is one of the rights granted under the GDPR. And since the GDPR applies to personal data processed in the EU (also if it concerns data subjects from outside the EU), the data subject could have the right to object to the processing. However, since this processing will be done to complete the (retail) contract, the right to object is likely not applicable.

35. Organizations are required to inform data subjects if the processing involves automated decision-making. Which of the following best describes automated decision-making?
   A. The use of quantum computing
   B. The review of CVs by the HR department
   C. **Criteria for selection programmed in by someone involved in the selection process (correct)**
   D. Use of audit software that automatically performs certain tests

Info:

C is the correct answer. This option results in decisions being made completely automated, meaning that no human judgment is involved beyond the point of programming the criteria.

36. Consent is one of the legal processing criteria that can be relied on. Which are the criteria for consent provided by a data subject?

  A. Reversible, written, machine-readable
  B. Provided by the parents of the data subject
  C. Explicit, freely given, specific (correct)
  D. A written and signed form with the date of consent

Info:

C is the correct answer. Article 7 of the GDPR describes the conditions for consent, which are reversible, explicit, feely given, and specific.

37. A data subject's request for erasure is not always honored. What could be a valid reason for refusal?

  A. There is a lawful processing criterion that prevents deletion of the personal data (correct)
  B. The amount of work it is for the controller can outweigh the data subject's right in most cases
  C. If the data subject has provided consent, the controller does not need to delete the personal data
  D. If the contract has been fulfilled, but the controller has an internal policy to keep the personal data for longer

Info:

A is the correct answer. If there is a lawful processing criterion, such as a legal obligation requiring processing of the personal data, then the controller cannot delete the personal data that is required to fulfill the legal obligation. Think of financial information the controller needs to keep due to certain tax regulations.

38. What is a possible privacy risk when combining several unrevealing data elements about someone?
   A. Unintentionally decrypting personal data
   B. Accidentally decompressing personal data
   C. The data can become corrupted
   D. The combining can result in profiling (correct)

Info:

D is the correct answer. Some things that are not revealing on their own can be revealing when combined. Think of a person's GPS information that shows him/her visiting an amusement park, combined with the HR records of that person calling in sick that day. By combining these two, it can be revealed that the person is committing fraud. Perhaps this is a farfetched example of profiling, but it illustrates the point.

39. An organization receives a request from a data subject to see all personal data the organization processes on him/her. Which of the following is most applicable?
   A. The request can be put on hold if the organization has financial issues
   B. Only unencrypted data needs to be provided
   C. The organization has to verify in its processes whether it processes any personal data on that person (correct)
   D. A data subject can oblige the organization to provide the personal data on a USB stick, so it is machine-readable

Info:

C is the correct answer. The organization is obliged to take a request seriously, and only when the organization established it is not processing personal data of that data subject can it stop looking.

40. How can the term "appropriate technical and organizational measures" best be described?
    A. A level of file protection appropriate for the risk
    B. Installing malware scanners for all computers, including those not connected to the internet
    C. Applying role-based access control, restricting every file to access by the CEO only
    D. A level of measures to protect the data appropriate for the risk (correct)

Info:

D is the correct answer. This term is commonly used, and simply refers to taking measures that are suitable for mitigating (solving/reducing) the risk. Technical in this context means technological, so equipment or software, and organizational can be interpreted as, for example, procedures and reporting structures. Option A might also sound correct, but only file protection is mentioned, making the answer incomplete.

41. Based on what is a controller most likely allowed to audit the processor it uses?
    A. The GDPR
    B. A data protection authority notice
    C. The data processing agreement (correct)
    D. The controller's authority

Info:

C is the correct answer. When a controller lets (part of) its processing be done by a processor, there will need to be a data processing agreement. This is an agreement in which the measures and responsibilities are listed, including the right for the controller to audit the processor. Auditing the processor can help the controller verify that the personal data is processed as agreed on in the data processing agreement, and some controllers include this requirement.

42. For large files that may cause an organization to run out of space, what would be an appropriate technical measure to prevent a data breach?
   A. Deleting files
   B. Removal of metadata
   C. Role-based access control
   D. Compression (correct)

Info:
D is the correct answer. Compression makes the files smaller, and thus saves space on the organization's server. If an organization would run out of space and as a result loses personal data (because of not being able to store it, or having to overwrite it), that could be considered a data breach.

43. For an organization with frequent staff changes, what would be an appropriate organizational measure to prevent a data breach?
   A. Complicated password requirements
   B. Appoint the role of the security officer to the data protection officer
   C. Require the staff to bring its own device
   D. Role-based access control (correct)

Info:
D is the correct answer. Role-based access control arranges access to files based on what role you have in an organization. The actual protection of the data with a control is arguably purely a technical measure, but defining and assigning the roles is an organizational measure, as is adopting the policy to use role-based access control. The phrasing is tricky here, but option D can also be reasoned to by realizing option A is counterproductive, option B is not appropriate, and option C brings more dangers than security.

44. A data processing agreement can be required before starting to process personal data. Which best describes a data processing agreement?
   A. An agreement the processor is obliged to let the controller sign before the controller starts processing personal data
   B. An agreement between the controller and processor detailing the level of security, as well as other details regarding the processing (correct)
   C. An agreement that makes agreements with sub-processors obsolete
   D. A document describing how data is processed in the different affiliates of a multi-national organization

Info:

B is the correct answer. The level of security and other details are what is included in a data processing agreement (although there is more to a data processing agreement).

45. Which most incorrectly describes a data processing impact assessment?
   A. A balancing of interests of the controller versus the data subjects (correct)
   B. A risk assessment
   C. An inventory of mitigated and unmitigated risks
   D. A (sometimes) mandatory assessment

Info:

A is the correct answer. This describes the balance that is performed for determining whether the "legitimate interest" lawful processing criterion can be relied on. The other three options are part of the definition/description of a data processing impact assessment.

46. The data protection officer has a special position in an organization. How can the position/role/job of the data protection officer not be described?
    A. Independent
    B. Working in the interest of the shareholder (correct)
    C. Reporting to the highest level of management
    D. Providing the data protection authority with information

Info:

B is the correct answer. The data protection officer is interested in the organization's compliance with the relevant privacy laws, and does not (and should not) have an interest in the shareholders. The only way the data protection officer works in the interest of the shareholders is to prevent fines and reputational damage as a consequence of poor privacy practices, but that should be seen as a consequence rather than a goal.

47. A data protection officer can be mandatory for an organization to appoint. In which case is it most likely that an organization needs to appoint a data protection officer?
    A. An average organization
    B. A US-based retailer
    C. A government-funded university (correct)
    D. A chemical research facility with over 250 staff members

Info:

C is the correct answer. Public bodies are required to have a data protection officer. When a university is government-funded, then it is potentially considered a public body, in which case a data protection officer is required. See Article 37 of the GDPR for the other categories that require a data protection officer.

48. What is the likely course of action after a data protection impact assessment has shown that some risks cannot be brought down to an acceptable level?
    A. Continue the processing regardless, as you have done all you can
    B. **Inform the Data Protection Authority (correct)**
    C. Inform the data subjects of the data breach
    D. Reserve budget for a fine

Info:

B is the correct answer. When a risk cannot be brought down to an acceptable level, which is a possible conclusion of the data protection impact assessment, the data protection authority can be informed about the processing and asked for permission. See recital 84 of the GDPR, which describes this.

49. Many organizations maintain a data processing inventory. What is the biggest benefit of performing a data processing inventory?
    A. **Being able to quickly see any processing that shares data elements with other processing (correct)**
    B. Being compliant with the GDPR
    C. Knowing where to direct the attention of the chief information security officer
    D. Being able to determine whether it is required to appoint a data protection officer

Info:

A is the correct answer. When creating the records of processing activities as required by article 30 of the GDPR (also referred to as the data processing inventory), it should become clear which processes use the same data elements. This is likely to happen because the tool you use for your data inventory (be it a simple spreadsheet or a complicated tool) is likely to make the connections/overlaps clear.

50. When a data subject complains to the data protection authority, the data protection authority can start an investigation. What is the most likely role of the organization's data protection officer in this case?
    A. Send the data protection authority the data on all the organization's employees
    B. The data protection officer is part of the investigation team
    C. Act as the point of contact for the data protection authority (correct)
    D. The data protection officer approves all the communication between the organization and the data protection authority

Info:

C is the correct answer. The data protection officer is likely the contact point of the data protection authority. Article 39 (1) (d) describes the data protection officer's duty to cooperate with the data protection authority (supervisory authority).

51. The Human Resources department of a company processes (sensitive) personal data. What is likely not appropriate processing of personal data?
    A. Receiving information from the company doctor about employees
    B. Using photographs of staff on the company website (correct)
    C. Process the sensitive personal data for social security purposes
    D. Process the sensitive personal data for wage payment purpose

Info:

B is the correct answer. The human resources department likely does not have a valid lawful processing criterion to use photographs on the website, except consent. Consent is problematic in this scenario since an employee who is asked for consent by his/her employer possibly feels pressured to consent, resulting in consent that is not freely given (and therefore not valid).

52. What is the issue/problem with asking employees for consent as an employer?
    A. The employer pays the employee
    B. Consent at work cannot be registered in the employee's file
    C. **The employees likely feel pressure to provide consent (correct)**
    D. There are limits to what consent can be asked for

Info:

C is the correct answer. An employee who is asked for consent by his/her employer possibly feels pressured to consent, resulting in consent that is not freely given (and therefore not valid).

This information can be used for the following four questions:

Due to a recent crisis, all education takes place online. In order to attend classes, students log on to a free video call service. The teacher then shares the lesson materials on the screen through the video call service and talks the students through the lesson.

Attendance is not monitored, because some parents objected to the processing. The school, scared by the parents and feeling pressured to accommodate for the sake of the students, decided students do not need to take part in the class live. Those students are allowed to download the recording of the class later.

53. In order to record the class, the school asks for the teachers' permission. What can be a difficulty in asking the teachers for permission?
   A. It will be impossible to get consent in writing
   B. Once the consent for the recordings is obtained, it cannot be withdrawn
   C. **The school is the teachers' employer, and the teachers might feel pressured (correct)**
   D. No possible other legal processing criterion is applicable

Info:
C is the correct answer. The school is the employer, and the teachers are the employees. An employee that is asked for consent by his/her employer possibly feels pressured to consent, resulting in consent that is not freely given (and therefore not valid).

54. If the students are willfully recorded by the school without disclosing it to the students or parents, and a data breach takes place resulting in the spread of a video of one of the students picking his nose, what is a possible scenario?
   A. The data protection authority forces the school to perform a data protection impact assessment to correct the breach
   B. **A claim based on Article 82 (correct)**
   C. Forced closure of the school
   D. Retroactive consent of the parents, rectifying the situation

Info:
B is the correct answer. If there is no lawful processing criterion, no privacy notice was provided, and parents were not asked to consent to the processing of their children's personal data, the processing is not legitimate. When the risks come to fruition through a data breach, the data subjects can likely prove that they suffered damages. Article 82 of the GDPR describes the right to compensation and liability.

55. Which of the following is not necessarily required before starting to process personal data in order to provide classes online?
   A. A lawful processing criterion
   B. A data protection impact assessment
   C. A privacy notice
   D. Consent (correct)

Info:

D is the correct answer. If, for example, there is a legal obligation to provide distance education and the personal data collected is minimized to that which is strictly necessary (so no unnecessary video of students and teachers), a different lawful processing criterion (other than consent) applies.

56. What would be an example of the proportionality principle in this case?
   A. Requiring parents to consent
   B. Performing a data protection impact assessment
   C. Requiring the use of software for which a data processing agreement is in place
   D. Not requiring students to turn on their camera (correct)

Info:

D is the correct answer. There is no point for the teachers to see the students, and especially not for the students to be recorded. Although there could be exceptions if it concerned an exam and the teacher needed to see whether the students were cheating and needed the camera for that reason.

57. Software can be installed that monitors the amount of data that leaves the network and intervenes when this seems excessive. What is this called?
   A. Leak fixing
   B. A policy control
   C. Data Loss Prevention (correct)
   D. Data breach reporting

Info:

C is the correct answer. This is called data loss prevention software, which can be useful to detect strange sorts/amounts of data being sent over the network, indicating potentially strange activity.

58. Which body/institution/organization do the directorates-general (departments) of the European Commission report with regards to data protection?
   A. The European Data Protection Supervisor (correct)
   B. The European Data Protection Board
   C. The Data Protection Agency in the country where the directorate-general is located
   D. The European Data Protection Authority

Info:

A is the correct answer. The European Data Protection Supervisor supervises the processing of personal data in the EU institutions, and the European Commission is one of the institutions of the EU. Be careful whenever the EDPS or one of the EU institutions is involved, because you will have to figure out whether the national data protection authority is involved, or the EDPS.

59. Of the following, which is the least fitting description of the European Data Protection Board?
   A. **The authority that supervises the national data protection authorities (correct)**
   B. The new version of the Working Party 29
   C. A collection of representatives of national data protection authorities
   D. An organization headquartered in Brussels

Info:

A is the correct answer. The EDPB does not supervise the national data protection authorities, but consists of (heads of) national data protection authorities. It is the replacement of the old Working Party 29. The EDPB issues advice but has no authority.

60. An organization delivers folders to a certain neighborhood. Which of the following is required?
   A. Legitimate interest
   B. **Respecting "no unaddressed mail" stickers (correct)**
   C. An opt-out opportunity
   D. An opt-in opportunity

Info:

B is the correct answer. The key here is that you understand that the organization likely delivers unaddressed folders, and therefore no EU privacy regulation applies since no personal data is processed. Option B is the only applicable option that remains, and there is no privacy law that requires the stickers "no unaddressed mail" to be respected (although there might be other laws, so this question is tricky and technically misleading, and option B is not necessarily correct but in the context of this exam the least incorrect).

61. Tracking technologies can help identify visitors that have also visited certain other websites. Which of the following is possibly a tracking technology?
    A. Analytical cookies
    B. Web beacons (correct)
    C. Functional cookies
    D. An HTTPS connection

Info:
B is the correct answer. Web beacons are usually transparent pixels that are loaded together with a website or e-mail (although they could, for example, also be part of an application). When this pixel is loaded, it is clear to the 'owner' of the web beacon which IP address has loaded the web beacon. An example could be a website containing a web beacon from a social media organization (and the website not being related to the social media organization). The visitor of the website would not see that the pixel is loaded, but the social media organization will know which IP address visited the website the web beacon was on. Web beacons are also referred to as tracking pixels. They are often from third parties, but not necessarily.

62. Personal use of personal data falls outside the scope of the General Data Protection regulation. Which of the following is most likely personal use of personal data?
    A. The use by a user of a social network website of family information (correct)
    B. The scraping of Twitter for scientific research
    C. A doctor giving a patient test results
    D. A company analyzing DNA at the request of individuals

Info:
A is the correct answer. The user itself is likely processing the data for personal use. Keep in mind that the organization behind the social network itself will also need to process the personal data (it needs to store it, at least), which is not considered personal use. So, the person's actions fall under personal use, but the maintenance of the social network itself is not personal use.

63. The data protection authority can investigate an organization. Which of the following is not a possible role of the data protection officer when the data protection authority is conducting an investigation?
    A. Being a contact person for the data protection authority
    B. Representing the organization (correct)
    C. Informing the CEO of the organization of the practices of the organization
    D. Performing data protection impact assessments to assess the situation

Info:

B is the correct answer. The data protection officer will never assume any responsibilities for the decisions taken for the organization, and in that sense will never represent the organization. It will be the contact person for the organization but never represent the organization. The similarity of options A and B should make you think about what the difference between these answers is, and how this difference can be relevant for the answer to this question.

64. Artificial Intelligence can be taught (or learn) to create datasets from publicly available information. Which of the following is the most likely privacy risk?
    A. Artificial Intelligence can use your personal data against you
    B. At a certain point, Artificial Intelligence will get out of control
    C. Artificial intelligence will not be able to determine whether something is personal data
    D. Newly generated data sets reveal new personal data (correct)

Info:

D is the correct answer. Perhaps it is farfetched with the current technological possibilities, but think for example of artificial intelligence being used to scan photos for certain physical aspects in public photographs that identify diseases the persons in the photographs have. Thus, generating new data is a risk.

This information can be used for the following four questions:

An international taxi company drives between Hungary, Serbia, and Croatia. The company has offices in all three countries, but the head office is located in Serbia.

The company focuses on business customers and mostly drives around clients within one of the three countries. However, international trips do occur, and the national offices communicate data of both drivers and customers with the head office.

At a certain point, an employee at the head office opens an attachment that asks the employee to log in with his company username and password. The employee didn't recognize this was a phishing attack and entered the information.

The party behind the phishing e-mail then used the employee's credentials to log on to the network of the taxi company.

65. After discovering what happened with the phishing e-mail, what should be the company's course of action?
   A. Report the breach to the data protection authority in Serbia
   B. Report the breach to the European Data Protection Supervisor
   C. Assess the situation and determine what exactly has been accessed (correct)
   D. Investigate and report to the relevant data protection authority after the investigation has finished

Info:
C is the correct answer. If the company is quick enough to prevent data from being accessed by external parties, there has not been a data breach (unless you count the loss of the employee's credentials as a data breach). In addition, if a data breach has taken place, the severity needs to be determined to assess whether, for example, the data subjects need to be informed.

66. To share the employee data and customer data with other branches, which of the following is required to allow the exchange?
   A. Privacy shield
   B. Data processing agreement
   C. Binding corporate rules (correct)
   D. A data protection impact assessment

Info:

C is the correct answer. Binding corporate rules concern the sharing of personal data within an organization in different countries. For an international organization, it can be necessary that the employee data and customer data are processed outside of the country in which they were collected, and in that case, binding corporate rules can be required (or the organization can choose standard contractual clauses). Privacy Shield is no longer acceptable, a data processing agreement would be required when external parties process for the organization (processors), and a data protection impact assessment merely assesses risks (and is not necessarily required).

67. Which would have the most impact on preventing the success of the phishing attack?
   A. Multi-factor authentication (correct)
   B. Scanning for viruses
   C. Scanning for malware
   D. Complicated passwords

Info:

A is the correct answer. Multi-factor authentication will require more than just a password and login, so a phishing attack (which usually aims to obtain that) is likely ineffective if multi-factor authentication has been properly set up.

68. The drivers use an application on their private phones to communicate regarding customers and use the navigation system to the destination. What is most recommended for the company to have in place for this specific situation?
    A. Opt-out possibilities for the driver
    B. Ensuring the use of the application is for the benefit of the driver
    C. Forcing the drivers to opt-in to the use of the application
    D. A bring your own device program (correct)

Info:
D is the correct answer. Although it will not mitigate the risks completely, a bring your own device program generally includes a policy on how employees' own devices can be used in a safe way. It is therefore recommended. Option A means nothing, as it can be seen as the same as not having a phone. Option B does not address any problem. Option C is problematic, as users should never be forced to opt-in.

69. New technologies can result in unforeseen privacy risks. Which of the following is the least likely to result in unforeseen privacy risks?
    A. Geolocation
    B. Biometric identification
    C. Mainframe storage (correct)
    D. CCTV

Info:
Option C is the correct answer. A mainframe is basically a large computer used by organizations to process large critical data streams (this is a short incomplete definition). Storing data on a mainframe does not result in any unforeseen privacy risks, and is not special (storage, whether for a milli-second or longer, is always required when processing personal data). The other options provide aspects that can result in risks that are less standard. Think of CCTV cameras that are positioned too invasively, biometric data that reveals too much, or geolocation data that records too much.

70. Before changing an aspect of work that could impact privacy, works councils are often asked for input. Which of the following is most likely a task of the works councils?
   A. Provide positive or negative advice (correct)
   B. To approve a strike
   C. Decide on which route to take
   D. Perform a data protection impact assessment

Info:

A is the correct answer. Works councils (in most EU countries) generally have to agree to something or provide advice. This advice is positive/negative/neutral. Strikes are approved by unions, decisions on the direction of an organization are up to management, and works councils are definitely not involved in data protection impact assessments (although they may want to study it to prepare for their advice).

71. Geolocation data can reveal where a device is at a certain time. When is geolocation most likely going to lead to processing personal data?
   A. When an organization keeps track of its cars (correct)
   B. When every device has a geolocation checker with no ID
   C. If geolocation is only active when a device is lost
   D. When a GPS device is used independently of vehicles

Info:

A is the correct answer. When cars are tracked with geolocation, it is also likely registered which employee is using that car. Because of that, the exact movements of that vehicle can be linked to one or more employees, likely resulting in the processing of personal data. C may also seem correct, but it is not necessarily revealing to know where a lost device is located (think, for example, of a device being lost somewhere in a warehouse).

72. In the US, the GDPR does not necessarily apply to direct marketing. Which law most likely applies to direct marketing in the US?
    A. CAN-SPAM (correct)
    B. POPI Act
    C. The e-privacy directive
    D. PIPEDA

Info:

A is the correct answer. CAN-SPAN (Controlling the Assault of Non-Solicited Pornography And Marketing) is the US act that applies. You will not need to know anything in-depth, but try to read up on the main laws, such as HIPAA, FACTA, and the California Consumer Privacy Act. For South Africa, it will be the POPI Act (Protection of Personal Information Act), and for Canada PIPEDA (Personal Information Protection and Electronic Documents Act).

73. When is marketing by regular mail least likely covered by the GDPR or e-privacy directive?
    A. When the mail is sent to the US
    B. When the mail is sent from an adequate country
    C. When the mail is sent unaddressed (correct)
    D. In case a prior business relationship exists

Info:

C is the correct answer. When mail is sent unaddressed, it does not fall under any privacy law, since there is (likely) no personal data processed in the process of sending the mail (since the mail is deposited in mail boxes without it being directed at one specific person or address).

74. The GDPR can be difficult to interpret, and organizations often require guidance. Where would the interpretation of the GDPR likely be discussed amongst data protection authorities?
    A. The investigations of the data protection authority
    B. The data protection authority conference
    C. The data protection officer meeting
    D. At meetings of the European Data Protection Board (correct)

Info:

D is the correct answer. The European Data Protection Board consists of representatives of the data protection authorities of the EU member states. This is the forum where they discuss issues amongst each other, which can result in issuing guidance.

75. What can be a reason to refuse a data portability request?
    A. There is a legitimate processing criterion in place
    B. A two-time extension has passed
    C. The controller refuses a valid form of identification in preference of another form of identification
    D. The data was not provided by the data subject (correct)

Info:

D is the correct answer. A data portability request only needs to be honored if the personal data was provided by the data subject himself/herself. In any other case, you can still request a copy of the personal data an organization processes, but it wouldn't be considered data portability.

76. Data is often collected without realizing that it concerns biometric data. Which of the following is least likely going to result in the collection of biometric data?
   A. A speed camera focused on the front of the car
   B. A chip in an identification card (correct)
   C. A temperature check at the entrance of an office building
   D. CCTV camera use

Info:

B is the correct answer. The chip in the ID card contains data, but this is not necessarily biometric data, and instead likely an ID number or access level. In that case, the card/chip is used to identify the person and not the biometric data. A speed camera likely still captures the image of someone, someone's temperature is biometric data, and CCTV cameras capture images of people.

77. The right to be forgotten can be used to force an organization to delete a data subject's personal data under certain conditions. Which of the following is an important consideration for an organization when receiving a request like that?
   A. Ensuring backups are taken into account (correct)
   B. Creating a barrier as high as possible
   C. Figuring out a new purpose and new lawful processing criterion to keep processing the data
   D. Requesting a fee for the deletion due to the amount of work

Info:

A is the correct answer. Organizations tend to forget that whatever data they process is possibly also part of a backup (if the organization creates regular backups). In that case, it has to be ensured that the personal data is deleted from the backup as well.

78. Canada is considered partially adequate. Which part of Canada is considered adequate?
    A. The government institutions
    B. The entire country, covered by Safe Harbor
    C. The French part of Canada
    D. The part covered by the Personal Information Protection and Electronic Documents Act (correct)
Info:

D is the correct answer. The non-governmental organizations in Canada are considered adequate. This is because the Personal Information Protection and Electronic Documents Act (PIPEDA) applies. The government in Canada is subject to different laws for the protection of personal data, which has not (yet) been deemed adequate.

79. An organization does not always process personal data itself. What kind of entities can ask other organizations to perform processing for them?
    A. Controllers
    B. Controllers or processors (correct)
    C. Sub-processors
    D. Organizations with an adequacy decision
Info:

B is the correct answer. This is phrased to mislead somewhat. Generally, a controller asks another organization (a processor) to process personal data on its behalf. However, the processor can in turn ask another organization to process (part of) the personal data it processes on behalf of the controller. The initial controller will remain the controller and will have to agree to the processor using another processor (sometimes referred to as a sub-processor). The sub-processor will also need to be part of the data processing agreement.

80. Organizations don't keep their data forever. What is a schedule on when to delete data also referred to as?
    A. **A data retention scheme (correct)**
    B. A data deletion policy
    C. A data policy
    D. A formatting scheme

Info:

A is the correct answer. This is the name for it. Important to remember here that the focus is on "retention", even though practically it specifies when data needs to be deleted.

81. When creating a data retention scheme, what is the least important consideration?
    A. **Whether the cloud server is of sufficient size (correct)**
    B. For which period the lawful processing criterion is applicable
    C. At which point the collection purpose has been achieved
    D. Which processes use the personal data

Info:

A is the correct answer. Size is important but the least important of the options provided because storage space is easily expanded. Options B, C, and D are important to determine when you legally need to delete the personal data.

82. Organizations outside the EU can process personal data on citizens of the EU. In which of the following situations does the GDPR most likely apply?
    A. **An Argentinian football club's international fan club (correct)**
    B. An American web shop
    C. A Canadian web shop
    D. The South African army

Info:

A is the correct answer. Since the fan club is international, it is likely targeting data subjects in the EU (in the sense that it facilitates their membership). This question can be tricky to answer since options B and C can under certain conditions also qualify. However, the "international" part of option A makes this the most likely answer.

83. Before processing personal data, the data subject has the right to be informed. Which of the following is not part of the information the controller is obliged to provide?
    A. **The exact data storage location (correct)**
    B. The retention period
    C. The lawful processing criterion
    D. The purpose for which the data is collected

Info:

A is the correct answer. Although the data subject is allowed to know in which country his/her personal data is stored, the exact storage location is not something that he/she has the right to know. Options B, C, and D are part of the information that needs to be provided to the data subject.

84. Organizations can create a set of binding corporate rules for international data transfers. What is not an aspect/property of binding corporate rules?
    A. It applies to both the EU and non-EU affiliates
    B. Standard contractual clauses are no longer required
    C. No deviations from the GDPR are included
    D. **A copy of the data processing inventory is included (correct)**

Info:
D is the correct answer. Binding corporate rules generally do not contain a copy of the data processing inventory. They can contain rules on its use, but generally do not contain a copy of it. Practically, the data processing inventory (or the records of processing) needs to be updated to reflect the current situation, so every time a new process starts the inventory needs to be updated, which is quite a hassle to attach to binding corporate rules.

85. Certain measures are not necessary if a country is considered adequate. Which institution/organization/body issues adequacy decisions?
    A. The European Parliament
    B. The European Data Protection Supervisor
    C. The European Data Protection Board
    D. **The European Commission (correct)**

Info:
D is the correct answer. The European Commission issues adequacy decisions. The approach to reaching an adequacy decision can be difficult to understand, but when a question appears on the exam on how adequacy decisions are issued it is your safest bet to choose the answer that involves at least the examination of the country's privacy laws.

This information can be used for the following three questions:

A real estate company that rents out apartments maintains an elaborate database of its tenants. The company owns many large apartment buildings, both in Romania and Hungary.

The tenants are citizens from all walks of life, and the real estate company stores the financial history of the tenant, indicating whether there have been payment issues in the past. Only the history of payments to the real estate agency is used to judge the tenants' financial reliability.

Naturally, the company processes large quantities of personal data. This is necessary for sending the right bill to the right tenant and arranging the necessary maintenance.

86. When potential tenants send their interest for a certain apartment, there is a box to tick in case they do not want to receive e-mails informing them of vacant apartments. What is this called?
    A. Opt-in
    B. Explicit consent for further processing
    C. **Opt-out (correct)**
    D. Irreversible

Info:

C is the correct answer. When you can choose not to take part in something, and action is required to indicate this, this is called opt-out. When the question was phrased in a way that required you to indicate that you wanted to be included (instead of excluded) this would be opt-in.

87. When the company sends e-mails to persons that did not tick the box not to receive further e-mails, what is the likely lawful processing criterion?
    A. Performance of a contract
    B. Consent
    C. Legitimate interest (correct)
    D. Vital interest

Info:
C is the correct answer. Whenever you are presented with options that all do not seem to apply, the most logical choice is legitimate interest. The assumption here is that, if the organization has balanced its interests and the privacy of the data subjects, and concluded they can send the e-mail, then the lawful processing criterion legitimate interest applies.

88. The agency uses CCTV in its buildings to protect the safety of the tenants. What is an important consideration in this case?
    A. Ensuring the cameras are not revealing the inside of the apartments (correct)
    B. Ensuring no activity in the elevator is revealed
    C. Ensuring all tenants are provided with the opportunity to opt-out
    D. Ensuring no children are filmed

Info:
A is the correct answer. If the cameras were directed at the inside of the apartments, it would be very revealing as it would be too invasive. Especially when it is possible to film enough for security, without filming the inside of apartments, this is preferred.

89. Social media organizations are known for providing tracking pixels. What is a use of these tracking pixels?
   A. **Targeted advertisement (correct)**
   B. Informing data subjects
   C. Linking of website to website
   D. Masking IP addresses

Info:

A is the correct answer. Social media organizations use tracking pixels they allow other websites to place, so they can register the websites their users visit. For example, if you visit a website for a certain pop group, and this pop group has a tracking pixel of a certain social media organization on its website, then the social media website would get a signal every time the tracking pixel is loaded (including by which IP address). The social media organization can then link that the user of the social media website/app with the corresponding IP address is interested in that pop group. The pop group, in return, can request the social media organization to advertise their music to users who have similar interests to the ones that already visited the pop group's website (which the social media organization knows because of the information it collected through the use of the tracking pixel). Complicated, hidden, and something useful for marketing departments, yet privacy-invasive for users.

90. What can most likely be a complicated privacy issue with whistleblower policies?
   A. **Protecting one identity can increase the likelihood of unjust harm to the other (correct)**
   B. There is no encryption sufficiently strong to be considered adequate
   C. Works council involvement
   D. The bureaucracy that follows can lead to mandatory disclosure of identity

Info:

A is the correct answer. Certain countries even forbid anonymous whistleblowing. If, for example, you dislike someone, it would be possible to fabricate a false accusation and anonymously scathe that person through the whistleblower program. A careful balancing of privacy and the other consequences is required.

Exam 2:

1. Which of the following is least likely to be required to take part in a data protection impact assessment?
   A. The privacy officer
   B. The security officer
   C. The data protection authority advisor
   D. The Chief Information Officer

2. A website has users upload data through the user's account. Which of the following is the most appropriate way of determining a data subject's identity in case of an access request?
   A. Contact through the account of the user
   B. A signed ID form
   C. A copy of the user's passport
   D. A video call

3. You buy a device from a web shop in the EU. The device only works with an application from a company outside of the EU. Which of the following is most likely true?
   A. The web shop is the controller
   B. The web shop is the processor
   C. The web shop is responsible for providing a privacy notice for the application
   D. The web shop is not responsible for the processing in the application

4. A health insurance company provides a data subject with a list of the data subject's current personal data. Which of the following has the health insurance company likely forgotten?
   A. To provide the personal data in machine-readable form
   B. To provide all mutations of the personal data
   C. To provide the data in a timely manner
   D. To post a privacy notice on its website

This information can be used for the following two questions:

In an apartment building, one neighbor makes a lot of noise around midnight every day. The noise consists of loud footsteps and something that sounds like weight-lifting equipment dropping on the floor.

Another neighbor is fed up with the noise and decides to take action. This neighbor is unable to determine from which apartment the noise is coming, so he writes a note which he puts up at the entrance of the building. The note reads "Since I don't think it is a good idea to knock on every door at midnight to ask where the noise is coming from, I would like to ask whoever the night owl is, to consider the sleep of the other neighbors."

The next night the noise continues. One of the neighbors writes to the landlord about the issue. The landlord then forwards the email to all tenants.

5. Which of the following would have respected the privacy of the complaining neighbor best?
   A. Install CCTV cameras
   B. Forward only the message, not the contact data
   C. Send all tenants an e-mail requesting them to stop making noise at midnight
   D. Visit the complaining neighbor, and visit all neighbors together

6. The noisy neighbor responds to the landlord, apologizing and claiming not to have been aware of the consequences of his actions. What can the landlord do?
   A. Forward the e-mail to the tenants, informing them the situation is solved
   B. Nothing, unless requested by the noisy neighbor, or if the noise continues
   C. Inform the tenants about the activities that caused the noise, however private
   D. Inform the tenants that the noise is due to the religious practice of the neighbor, and there is nothing he can do

7. A car spotter takes photographs of fancy cars that pass his apartment and stores them in his collection. What security measures does the GDPR likely require the car spotter to take?
   A. A virus scanner
   B. None, the activity is outside the scope
   C. Regular software updates
   D. An encrypted SD card in the camera

8. After BREXIT, what did the United Kingdom stop to be?
   A. A member state
   B. A safe country
   C. A European country
   D. A tax-paying country

9. In case the United Kingdom does not receive an adequacy decision, which of the following is not a way to transfer personal data?
   A. Binding Corporate Rules
   B. Standard contractual clauses
   C. A data protection impact assessment
   D. Model clauses

10. In case a controller in the EU obtained consent from data subjects in the United Kingdom before BREXIT, what happens with this consent post-BREXIT?
    A. The conditions change, and new consent needs to be provided
    B. The consent transitions into legitimate interest
    C. The processing must be stopped
    D. The consent remains valid

11. The GDPR is a comprehensive law. Which of the following is another example of a comprehensive law?
    A. HIPAA
    B. POPI
    C. CAN-SPAM
    D. FACTA

12. A certain device requires you to provide consent before it functions. Which of the following requirements for consent is most likely not respected?
    A. Explicit
    B. Clear
    C. Freely given
    D. Reversible

13. An organization asks you to sign a waiver for any damages, including damages related to data protection. Which GDPR article are they most likely referring to?
    A. Article 9
    B. Article 82
    C. Article 35
    D. Article 6

14. A video game shows an advertisement based on the user's in-game behavior, linked to his/her ID/profile. Which of the following is least likely the case?
    A. Since it is a video game, the user profile cannot contain personal data
    B. When a profile is created, and information is linked to it, it is personal data
    C. The user should have been provided an opportunity to opt-out
    D. The advertisements are placed, relying on the legitimate interest lawful processing criterion

15. An online forum where people discuss a variety of topics keeps track of when users are active and also keeps track of their actions. The webmaster systematically checks the logs. What can this perhaps be called?
    A. Consent
    B. Surveillance
    C. Unsolicited advertisement
    D. Targeted advertisement

16. A script that learns improvements, and adapts, what can that likely be called?
    A. Internet of things
    B. Artificial intelligence
    C. Tracking cookies
    D. Quantum computing

17. If you are shown advertisements based on what you have entered into a search engine, what can this be called?
    A. Selective screening
    B. Search engine marketing
    C. Ad screening
    D. Target selection

18. During a visit to your favorite web shop, you see the message "you might also like". What is likely used to make this possible?
    A. Cookies
    B. Quantum computing
    C. A script injector
    D. Data mining

19. Multi-factor authentication can be an effective security measure. Which of the following is an example?
    A. Asking two passwords
    B. Logging in on specific mainframes
    C. Fingerprint authentication
    D. Iris scan

20. A company in China wants to process personal data from EU data subjects. Which of the following is possibly the case?
    A. An adequacy decision is required for China
    B. If the data subjects were not targeted, the GDPR rules do not have to be followed
    C. China will have to first implement a new law
    D. Processing personal data in China will never be allowed

21. You are applying for a job in the same organization you worked for fifteen years ago. The company rejects your application based on your last performance appraisal it has on file from fifteen years ago. Which of the following is most likely applicable?
    A. The company can keep the performance appraisal because the lawful processing criterion legitimate interest is applicable
    B. The only way the company would have been allowed to keep the performance appraisal for fifteen years is valid consent
    C. An organization can keep performance appraisals as long as it wants because it is its own creation
    D. The applicant is not allowed to see the performance appraisal

This information can be used for the following four questions:

Unexpectedly, you receive the news that you won a prize in a raffle. You do not remember having signed up for the raffle, so you investigate.

It turns out the online retailer where you purchased a sweater five years ago, has entered your e-mail address in the raffle. Your positive surprise turns into amazement at the retailer's audacity.

The next day you decide to send an access request since you want to know what exactly the retailer still processes. You receive a negative response, claiming the retailer opted to delete your personal data instead.

22. In order to keep your e-mail address for as long as the retailer has, which of the following is required?
    A. Legitimate interest
    B. A retroactive contract
    C. A valid lawful processing criterion
    D. A data protection impact assessment

23. The retailer deleted your personal data. Which of the following is likely applicable?
    A. The retailer should have requested the data protection authority's advice
    B. The retailer was not allowed to delete your personal data when you requested it
    C. The retailer should have requested the data protection authority's permission
    D. The retailer has a legitimate interest in keeping the inner workings of his business confidential, hence the deletion is justified

24. If, apart from using the e-mail address for the raffle, the e-mail address is part of the invoice, which of the following lawful processing criteria is likely applicable?
    A. Required to comply with a legal obligation
    B. Necessary for the performance of a contract
    C. Legitimate interest of the data subject
    D. Legitimate interest of the controller

25. What did the online retailer have to do at the very least before entering your e-mail address in the raffle?
    A. Increase security
    B. Update the privacy notice, and send it to you
    C. Migrate to a cloud-based solution
    D. Perform a data protection impact assessment

26. Sensitive personal data is covered under Article 9 of the GDPR. How can sensitive personal data best be described?
    A. Personal data that is manifestly made public
    B. Personal data that has been obtained by data mining a large number of transactions
    C. Personal data that generally requires a higher level of protection, and a condition to be met beyond Article 6
    D. Personal data for which a data protection impact assessment is always required

27. You request your personal data from an organization, and find out your address is incorrect despite having updated it. Which of the following is likely the case?
    A. The integrity principle has been compromised
    B. The lawful processing criterion has become void
    C. The organization will automatically receive a fine
    D. The accuracy principle has not been respected

28. Which of the following would likely not be considered an establishment in the EU or targeting EU citizens?
    A. An online retailer based in the US, selling printed flags on demand, including those of EU member states
    B. A Canadian online retailer allowing for payment in Croatian currency
    C. An online retailer based in Greece, focusing on the US market
    D. A local grocery store on the border with the EU, selling EU products cheaper, using price tags in the language of the EU country it borders with

29. An online retailer where you have complained in the past still has a record of your complaints. Where would you have expected to be informed about this practice?
    A. In the privacy notice, before sending a complaint
    B. In the sales contract, at the time of ordering
    C. On the website of the retailer, after submitting the order form
    D. In the privacy notice, before placing an order

30. Organizations do not always respect the principle of purpose limitation. Of the following, which is an example?
    A. Storing the gathered personal data in several systems, including on a backup
    B. Processing personal data in several affiliates of the organization
    C. Placing an e-mail address, gathered in the context of a sale, on a mailing list
    D. Storing information about the processing in the data processing inventory

31. Which of the following least likely requires a data processing agreement?
    A. An accountancy firm handling your business' taxes
    B. A cloud provider, hosting your organization's backup
    C. An organization, processing publicly available social media data your organization has mined
    D. A bakery, sending your employees a Christmas bread

32. The data protection authority needs to be notified in certain cases. Of the following, which is least likely a data breach?
    A. An e-mail sent to the wrong addressee
    B. An external hard drive that was lost
    C. Processing that was not mentioned in the privacy notice
    D. A stolen laptop

33. The term "appropriate technical and organizational measures" can seem like a vague concept. Which of the following best describes this concept?
    A. A privacy policy adopted to the financial means allocated by the CEO
    B. Full encryption on backups
    C. Role-based access control
    D. A context-dependent level of security measures

34. Awareness within an organization is created least effectively with which of the following?
    A. A privacy policy of the organization
    B. Employee training for a large part of the staff
    C. A security policy
    D. A privacy notice on the website

35. Of the following, which person is least desirable to sign a data processing agreement on the controller side?
    A. The CIO
    B. The data protection officer
    C. The CEO
    D. The procurement manager

36. A data breach notification can be required in case of a data breach. Who in an organization is responsible for the data breach notification being sent?
    A. The CISO
    B. The data protection officer
    C. The privacy officer
    D. The CEO

37. For which of the following is consent least likely required?
    A. Data pertaining to children
    B. Sensitive financial data, regarding bankruptcy
    C. Fingerprints
    D. Observable biometric data

38. In which of the following was the European Economic Area established?
    A. The Agreement on the European Economic Area
    B. The treaty of Lisbon
    C. The treaty of Vienna
    D. The treaty of Milan

39. It is not always clear whether something can indirectly lead to uncovering new personal data. Which of the following will most likely lead to the unintended uncovering of sensitive personal data?
    A. The loss of a credit card, found by wrongdoers
    B. Malware, uncovering all technical aspects of your computer
    C. A strike, where members of a union decide to collectively go on strike
    D. An online survey, without open-text fields

40. Prior to the GDPR, there was the Data Protection Directive. Which of the following is generally not a difference between a Directive and a Regulation?
    A. Regulations require member states to implement its requirements but leave more freedom than a Directive
    B. Fewer requirements of a Regulation are open to a different extent of implementation
    C. Directives lay aims for the member states, Regulations are applied in their entirety
    D. A Directive needs to be implemented into law, whereas a regulation does not

41. A processor has purchased a new type of security software after starting to work for a new client. What is this likely the direct result of?
    A. A GDPR requirement
    B. A condition in the privacy notice
    C. The processor's privacy policy
    D. A clause in the data processing agreement

42. One of the lawful processing criteria is "necessary for the performance of a contract". What best describes this?
    A. An address is always needed to complete a contract, which can be considered personal data
    B. The details specified in the contract regarding all the data subject's part of the processing
    C. A piece of information from the data subject, without which it can reasonably be expected that part of the contract cannot be completed
    D. A contract specifying appropriate technical and organizational measures for processing

43. Social media organizations can make web beacons available. Of the following, which best describes the likely process?
  A. The user agrees to a transparent process of tracking all over the web
  B. A tracking cookie is installed, uploading the full browser history to the social media organization for advertisement purposes
  C. Once the user clicks on the web beacon, it registers the visit to the social media organization
  D. A transparent pixel is placed on any website, and when that website is visited, that visit is registered by the social media organization

44. In the past, many employers monitored their employees' online behavior. If, nowadays, an employer has access to its employees' browser history, what is likely required?
  A. A bring your own device policy
  B. A secure server for storing user data
  C. A data protection impact assessment
  D. A valid lawful processing criterion and a privacy notice

45. When placing CCTV cameras in a building, which of the following is likely the least important consideration?
  A. When the camera is pointed at the entrance, it could reveal the late arrival of employees
  B. When the camera is pointed at a hallway containing restroom doors, it could reveal sensitive personal data
  C. When the camera is pointed at someone's desk, this could be disproportionate
  D. The retention of the recordings could require a strict policy

46. When claiming damages from a violation of the GDPR, what is required?
    A. A mental breakdown due to the complicatedness of a privacy notice
    B. To be able to show a form of damage as a consequence of a violation of the GDPR
    C. The stress caused after finding out what exactly an organization knows/processes
    D. The result of a data protection authority investigation needs to be present in court, to prove damages

47. Data protection officers have a special place in an organization. Of the following, which is least likely true?
    A. The data protection officer is the highest level of management in the organization
    B. The CEO can overrule the data protection officer
    C. The data protection officer is not required to be part of the data protection impact assessment team
    D. A data protection officer is never mandatory

48. Regarding the right to be forgotten, which of the following is true?
    A. An organization does not necessarily have to stop processing your personal data
    B. An organization is always required to request extensive identification
    C. The personal data is not required to be deleted from low-risk backups
    D. The data protection officer is responsible for the deletion

49. Sometimes the data subjects need to be notified of a data breach. In which of the following is a notification least likely required?
    A. The leak of a large list of partially masked IP addresses of a certain website
    B. A misaddressed e-mail, containing a message regarding the dietary preferences of several people
    C. A list of students' grades being posted online publicly, contrary to university policy
    D. A backup server running without password protection for a few days

50. Students hack into their political science professor's computer and steal the exam before exam day. Which of the following is most likely true?
    A. The professor intended to publish the exam, therefore it can be considered manifestly made public
    B. If the exam composed by the professor contains the professor's political views, the exam should be considered sensitive personal data
    C. As soon as the professor finds out, the data subjects are required to be informed
    D. The professor can claim damages from the university based on Article 82 of the GDPR

51. Personal data can be made anonymous or pseudonymous. Which if the following is not correct?
    A. No protection is required for anonymous data
    B. Strict protection can be required for pseudonymous data
    C. A separate set of information can be used to reverse pseudonymous data
    D. They are both reversible

52. You download a list of names and occupations from a website. After you replace the names with numbers, which of the following is most likely true?
   A. The new list no longer contains personal data
   B. The new list contains anonymous data
   C. The new list contains pseudonymous data
   D. The public data was never personal data

53. If a controller intends to keep personal data for a longer period than needed, which data processing principle is likely not respected?
   A. Storage limitation
   B. Proportionality
   C. Accuracy
   D. Integrity

54. If a processor wants to use personal data it initially collected for a controller for its own purposes, which data protection principle is likely not respected?
   A. Proportionality
   B. Storage limitation
   C. Accuracy
   D. Purpose limitation

55. Which lawful processing criterion requires a controller to do the most analysis?
   A. Contractual necessity
   B. Consent
   C. Legal obligation
   D. Legitimate interest

56. Of the following, which is not a condition for consent?
   A. Freely given
   B. Written
   C. Specific
   D. Reversible

57. A controller has obtained consent for placing a customer on a mailing list after a sale. The data subject then notifies the controller he/she no longer consents. What does the controller need to do?
   A. Delete all personal data of the data subject
   B. Provide a copy of all personal data to the data subject
   C. Update the privacy notice
   D. Stop processing the personal data for the mailing list

58. Regarding informing data subjects about third parties, which of the following is not true?
   A. It needs to be explicit that third parties are involved
   B. Data subjects need to be informed about third parties before the processing starts
   C. The names of the third parties need to be mentioned
   D. Third parties outside of the EU might require additional measures

59. Trolling bots are actively bothering people on social media websites. What are these trolling bots possibly?
   A. Internet of things
   B. Malware
   C. Script kiddies
   D. Artificial intelligence

60. Of the following, which is the least comprehensive law?
   A. CAN-SPAM
   B. POPI
   C. PIPEDA
   D. GDPR

61. Of the following, which is an example of self-regulation?
   A. PCI-DS
   B. A directive
   C. A regulation
   D. A member state's national law

62. Everyone's online presence leaves a mark. What is it called when advertisers seek you out because of this?
    A. Social media advertising
    B. Cookie analysis
    C. Online behavioral advertising
    D. Online tracking

63. An organization refuses to issue company phones, yet requires employees to own a phone to make emergency phone calls. What can this likely be called?
    A. Illegitimate processing
    B. Legitimate interest
    C. Consent not freely given
    D. Bring your own device

64. Spreadsheet applications do not have to be loaded from a user's hard drive, but can also be loaded from an external server. What can this be called?
    A. A cloud server
    B. Software as a service
    C. An encrypted connection
    D. External data processing

65. How can you best describe the role of the European Data Protection Board?
    A. Litigate
    B. Investigate
    C. Legislate
    D. Guide

66. Employees need to know how management intends to translate data protection requirements into action. Where will the staff most likely find this information?
    A. The GDPR
    B. Procedures
    C. The organization's privacy notice
    D. Advice from the data protection officer

67. There are multiple ways of safeguarding personal data in international data processing. For processing EU personal data by a processor in an adequate country, which of the following is needed?
    A. Nothing, as the country is adequate
    B. A data processing agreement
    C. Binding corporate rules and a data processing agreement
    D. Binding corporate rules

68. Data processors can be required to cooperate with the data protection authority's investigation in case of a data breach. In case the processor does not cooperate due to a clause missing in the data processing agreement, who is responsible?
    A. The processor has its own responsibility, based on the GDPR
    B. The responsibility for data breaches is agreed on in the data processing agreement
    C. The controller is responsible for ensuring the processing is done safely
    D. The data subject is informed in the privacy notice if the controller distances itself from responsibility for data breaches

69. How can the European Data Protection Supervisor best be described?
    A. The data protection authority of the institutions of the EU
    B. Representing the member states' data protection authorities
    C. The EU data protection authorities' coordination body
    D. The only authority to impose fines

70. Privacy by design has become a requirement in the GDPR. Which of the following best describes privacy by design?
    A. A method/principle to embed privacy in the product/processing
    B. A way to turn off all tracking and stay anonymous
    C. Required program settings, so you can opt-out of any processing of personal data
    D. Compatibility with privacy-protecting browser settings

71. Where does privacy by design start?
    A. At the layout design phase
    B. At the testing phase
    C. As early as possible
    D. At the data protection officer's approval

72. You are an employee of one of the institutions of the EU. You audit the European Commission. Which institution are you most likely working for?
    A. The parliament
    B. The European Court of Auditors
    C. The European External Action Service
    D. The Council of Europe

73. A data protection impact assessment can be mandatory for certain processing. Which of the following best describes the outcome of a data protection impact assessment?
    A. A security standard for risky processing
    B. A way for the data protection officer to communicate his/her opinion
    C. A collaborative document from both management and the data protection officer
    D. An inventory of risks and mitigative measures

74. Multinational organizations will have to fall under a data protection authority. Under which data protection authority will a multinational organization likely fall?
    A. The trans-EU data protection authority
    B. The local ombudsman
    C. The ambassador's data protection authority
    D. The data protection authority of the country of its head office in the EU

75. In case an employee is new to an organization and receives an access request, what is the best place to start?
    A. A data processing inventory
    B. Data protection impact assessments
    C. The privacy policy
    D. The organization's cloud backup

76. An organization's management does not always welcome the advice of the data protection officer. What can management do when it disagrees with the data protection officer?
    A. Move the person who is the data protection officer to a different role
    B. Perform a data protection impact assessment with a different team in order to get a different outcome
    C. Continue with the planned processing regardless
    D. Leave the processing out of the data processing inventory

77. The EU consists of institutions and bodies. Which of the following is not one of the EU's institutions?
    A. European Central Bank
    B. Council of the EU
    C. European Commission
    D. Council of Europe

78. Processors at times hire third parties to process for them. If that processor hires another third party to process on behalf of them, what is that third party called?
   A. A third-party responsible
   B. A controller
   C. A processor
   D. A sub-controller

This information can be used for the following four questions:

A mental health coaching firm has recently started conducting its activities online. Not only can clients book in-person appointments, but coaching sessions can also take place through an internet connection, from the comfort of the client's home.

Clients are requested to download a video calling application, either on their phone or on their computer. The application was chosen by the organization, as it is the only application compatible with its hardware.

Not all clients are comfortable in front of the camera. Unfortunately, the application does not have the option to disable the video stream. Because of this, several clients have pointed the camera away from them.

For clients, the software is free to use, but the coaching firm pays a subscription for a certain number of consecutive calls at a time. Practically this means one license per coach.

79. Given that the video cannot be disabled by the client, what is most clearly not respected?
   A. Transparency
   B. Privacy notice
   C. Privacy by design
   D. Specific consent

80. Since the coaching firm chose the video software, what is the company that sells/hosts/maintains the software?
    A. A controller
    B. A processor
    C. An external partner
    D. A co-responsible

81. Based on the nature of the activities of the coaching company, combined with the new video calling practice, which of the following would you consider the biggest risk?
    A. The data processing agreement does not contain a clause about sub-processors
    B. No approval for the new method has been provided by the data protection officer
    C. A data breach is likely to occur when clients record the sessions
    D. Sensitive personal data is processed without adequate technical and organizational measures

82. Regarding the video stream the coaches use, what is the most likely applicable lawful processing criterion?
    A. Legitimate interest, provided that clients are able to turn their camera away
    B. Contract, as the clients have a contract with the coaching firm
    C. Vital interest, since the coaching can concern mental issues
    D. Consent, because the processing cannot commence without consent

This information can be used for the following five questions:

You build and host websites. The content of these websites is dictated by your customers. Your customers range from individuals with hobby websites to small business owners' websites.

The websites can be simple and purely informational, or complex and significantly interactive. This leads to visitors loading information only, or loading and leaving information.

Recently, more and more customers are requesting you to sign a contract detailing the security and reporting requirements. This is a big hassle, and in order to reduce your workload, you ask your customers to sign a standard contract you composed yourself.

83. What is the contract referred to above called?
    A. A sub-processor contract
    B. A data protection impact assessment
    C. A data transfer agreement
    D. A data processing agreement

84. What would you call the visitor of a website in case the visit is interactive?
    A. A processor
    B. A data subject
    C. A co-controller
    D. A sub-processor

85. One of your customers instructs you to place a transparent pixel on sections of its website, in order to log which IP address opened which section at which time. What is this pixel called?
    A. A tracking frame
    B. A pixel query
    C. A web beacon
    D. An analytical cookie

86. In the case of the transparent pixel, which principle is likely violated when logging these details?
    A. Transparency
    B. Accuracy
    C. Integrity and confidentiality
    D. Proportionality

87. In this case, when you hire a company to do part of the work for you because your clients are too demanding, what are you?
    A. A processor
    B. A controller
    C. A sub-processor
    D. A co-controller

88. In which of the following situations would binding corporate rules be most appropriate?
    A. An organization in the EU cooperating with a private organization in Canada, exchanging employee personal data
    B. A government organization using contractors in several countries outside of the EU
    C. An organization with affiliates in Germany and Bahrain, not exchanging sensitive personal data
    D. When using a processor in the US, assuming there is a suitable replacement for Privacy Shield

89. Some processing of sensitive personal data is not restricted. Of the following, which is most likely restricted?
    A. Churches maintaining a member list of their members' religion
    B. Employers processing union membership of their employees
    C. A doctor processing medical data
    D. The processing of a national identification number by the tax services

90. Which principle does role-based access control protect most?
    A. Storage limitation
    B. Proportionality
    C. Purpose limitation
    D. Confidentiality

Answer key exam 2:
1C, 2A, 3D, 4B, 5C, 6B, 7B, 8A, 9C, 10D, 11B, 12C, 13B, 14A,
15B, 16B, 17B, 18A, 19B, 20B, 21B, 22C, 23B, 24A, 25B, 26C,
27D, 28A, 29D, 30C, 31A, 32C, 33D, 34D, 35B, 36D, 37B, 38A,
39C, 40A, 41D, 42C, 43D, 44D, 45A, 46B, 47A, 48A, 49A, 50B,
51D, 52C, 53A, 54D, 55D, 56B, 57D, 58C, 59D, 60A, 61A, 62C,
63D, 64B, 65D, 66B, 67B, 68C, 69A, 70A, 71C, 72B, 73D, 74D,
75A, 76C, 77D, 78C, 79C, 80B, 81D, 82A, 83D, 84B, 85C, 86D,
87A, 88C, 89B, 90D

Correct answers and explanations for exam 2:
1. Which of the following is least likely to be required to take
   part in a data protection impact assessment?
   A. The privacy officer
   B. The security officer
   C. The data protection authority advisor (correct)
   D. The Chief Information Officer

Info:
C is the correct answer. A data protection impact assessment is
something that takes place within the organization. The data
protection authority might, at some point, be informed of risky
processing of personal data within an organization, but it will not
take part in the data protection impact assessment.

2. A website has users upload data through the user's account.
   Which of the following is the most appropriate way of
   determining a data subject's identity in case of an access
   request?
   A. Contact through the account of the user (correct)
   B. A signed ID form
   C. A copy of the user's passport
   D. A video call

Info:
A is the correct answer. Access through the user's account is
relatively reliable and non-invasive. A video call would be quite
invasive, and a copy of the user's passport or signing a form is less
reliable (it is easier to fake a signature or steal a password than it is
to hack a secure password).

3. You buy a device from a web shop in the EU. The device only works with an application from a company outside of the EU. Which of the following is most likely true?
   A. The web shop is the controller
   B. The web shop is the processor
   C. The web shop is responsible for providing a privacy notice for the application
   D. The web shop is not responsible for the processing in the application (correct)

Info:
D is the correct answer. Although the web shop sells the device, the web shop is not the controller (the web shop only sells and does not produce the device). Who the controller is depends on who is in control of the software that needs to be used, and who determines that this specific software needs to be used.

4. A health insurance company provides a data subject with a list of the data subject's current personal data. Which of the following has the health insurance company likely forgotten?
   A. To provide the personal data in machine-readable form
   B. To provide all mutations of the personal data (correct)
   C. To provide the data in a timely manner
   D. To post a privacy notice on its website

Info:
B is the correct answer. If the health care provider also has old personal data, or has a registration of how the data subject's personal data has changed over time, this itself is also personal data and (likely) needs to be provided when requested.

This information can be used for the following two questions:

In an apartment building, one neighbor makes a lot of noise around midnight every day. The noise consists of loud footsteps and something that sounds like weight-lifting equipment dropping on the floor.

Another neighbor is fed up with the noise and decides to take action. This neighbor is unable to determine from which apartment the noise is coming, so he writes a note which he puts up at the entrance of the building. The note reads "Since I don't think it is a good idea to knock on every door at midnight to ask where the noise is coming from, I would like to ask whoever the night owl is, to consider the sleep of the other neighbors."

The next night the noise continues. One of the neighbors writes to the landlord about the issue. The landlord then forwards the email to all tenants.

5. Which of the following would have respected the privacy of the complaining neighbor best?
   A. Install CCTV cameras
   B. Forward only the message, not the contact data
   C. **Send all tenants an e-mail requesting them to stop making noise at midnight (correct)**
   D. Visit the complaining neighbor, and visit all neighbors together

Info:
C is the correct answer. Option C is least likely to expose the identity of the individual that has complained of options B, C, and D. Therefore, it is the preferred option. CCTV is too invasive, as it will reveal more than just the noise, and if the problem can be solved in a less invasive way than by installing CCTV the less invasive solution should have the preference.

6. The noisy neighbor responds to the landlord, apologizing and claiming not to have been aware of the consequences of his actions. What can the landlord do?
   A. Forward the e-mail to the tenants, informing them the situation is solved
   B. Nothing, unless requested by the noisy neighbor, or if the noise continues (correct)
   C. Inform the tenants about the activities that caused the noise, however private
   D. Inform the tenants that the noise is due to the religious practice of the neighbor, and there is nothing he can do

Info:

B is the correct answer. No more information than necessary should be shared about any of the persons involved, both about the complaining neighbor and about the person making the noise. In this case, if the problem doesn't continue, the landlord shouldn't do more (from a privacy perspective).

7. A car spotter takes photographs of fancy cars that pass his apartment and stores them in his collection. What security measures does the GDPR likely require the car spotter to take?
   A. A virus scanner
   B. None, the activity is outside the scope (correct)
   C. Regular software updates
   D. An encrypted SD card in the camera

Info:

B is the correct answer. The person does this for personal use and the processing is there for outside of the scope of the GDPR. If the car spotter were to upload the photos to websites of collectors where the photos are published, it would fall under the scope of the GDPR.

8. After BREXIT, what did the United Kingdom stop to be?
   A. A member state (correct)
   B. A safe country
   C. A European country
   D. A tax-paying country

Info:

A is the correct answer. The countries that are part of the EU are referred to as member states. Since the United Kingdom left the EU, it is no longer a member state (of the EU).

9. In case the United Kingdom does not receive an adequacy decision, which of the following is not a way to transfer personal data?
   A. Binding Corporate Rules
   B. Standard contractual clauses
   C. A data protection impact assessment (correct)
   D. Model clauses

Info:

C is the correct answer. A data protection impact assessment is not linked to the international transfer of personal data (although international transfer could make the processing riskier, in which case it would be required to perform a data protection impact assessment to assess the risks involved).

10. In case a controller in the EU obtained consent from data subjects in the United Kingdom before BREXIT, what happens with this consent post-BREXIT?
    A. The conditions change, and new consent needs to be provided
    B. The consent transitions into legitimate interest
    C. The processing must be stopped
    D. The consent remains valid (correct)

Info:

D is the correct answer. When personal data is processed within the EU, the GDPR applies regardless of the country of the data subject. Therefore, it doesn't matter whether the data subject is in the EU or not (as is the case with the United Kingdom after BREXIT). This question aims to confuse you by making you think the rules in the United Kingdom itself are relevant for this question, which is not the case (although there could be stricter rules in the United Kingdom at some point, but for your exam just expect questions like this one to pertain to the GDPR).

11. The GDPR is a comprehensive law. Which of the following is another example of a comprehensive law?
    A. HIPAA
    B. POPI (correct)
    C. CAN-SPAM
    D. FACTA

Info:

B is the correct answer. POPI (Protection of Personal Information Act) is the data protection law of South Africa, which is quite similar to the GDPR. The GDPR is comprehensive, and POPI is comprehensive. These are details you should remember because there will be a small number of questions like this. Remembering details such as this one should not have your priority if you don't have much time to prepare, but if you have plenty of time small details that may not seem relevant are worth remembering.

12. A certain device requires you to provide consent before it functions. Which of the following requirements for consent is most likely not respected?
    A. Explicit
    B. Clear
    C. Freely given (correct)
    D. Reversible

Info:

C is the correct answer. If you need to consent to the processing of your personal data before a device works, it is choosing between a device that doesn't function and losing privacy. This is not really a free choice, hence the consent is likely not completely freely given.

13. An organization asks you to sign a waiver for any damages, including damages related to data protection. Which GDPR article are they most likely referring to?
    A. Article 9
    B. Article 82 (correct)
    C. Article 35
    D. Article 6

Info:

B is the correct answer. This is Article 82 of the GDPR. Be sure to remember the important articles of the GDPR (such as 6 with the lawful processing criteria, 9 regarding sensitive personal data, etc.).

14. A video game shows an advertisement based on the user's in-game behavior, linked to his/her ID/profile. Which of the following is least likely the case?
   A. **Since it is a video game, the user profile cannot contain personal data (correct)**
   B. When a profile is created, and information is linked to it, it is personal data
   C. The user should have been provided an opportunity to opt-out
   D. The advertisements are placed, relying on the legitimate interest lawful processing criterion

Info:

A is the correct answer. Even in a video game, all information that says anything about an identifiable individual can be considered personal data. Here, whether the video game is online or not, there are likely aspects that (especially when combined) identify the player of the game that are unique enough to trace back to a single person (nickname, e-mail, computer configuration, etc.).

15. An online forum where people discuss a variety of topics keeps track of when users are active and also keeps track of their actions. The webmaster systematically checks the logs. What can this perhaps be called?
   A. Consent
   B. **Surveillance (correct)**
   C. Unsolicited advertisement
   D. Targeted advertisement

Info:

B is the correct answer. The webmaster systematically checks the logs, which can be seen as systematic monitoring. Surveillance can be said to be a form of systematic monitoring. See Article 35(3)(c) of the GDPR, as a data protection impact assessment might be required.

16. A script that learns improvements, and adapts, what can that likely be called?
    A. Internet of things
    B. Artificial intelligence (correct)
    C. Tracking cookies
    D. Quantum computing

Info:

B is the correct answer. Artificial intelligence is the display of intelligence by a machine. This is a script that learns (which a machine runs), therefore it fits the definition of artificial intelligence.

17. If you are shown advertisements based on what you have entered into a search engine, what can this be called?
    A. Selective screening
    B. Search engine marketing (correct)
    C. Ad screening
    D. Target selection

Info:

B is the correct answer. Certain search engines store your searches and use these to create a profile of you. This profile is then used to provide you with targeted advertisements. Be sure to check the privacy settings of the search engine you're using. In addition, using a VPN program can change your IP address, making it more difficult for a search engine to link your searches to only you.

18. During a visit to your favorite web shop, you see the message "you might also like". What is likely used to make this possible?
    A. **Cookies (correct)**
    B. Quantum computing
    C. A script injector
    D. Data mining

Info:

A is the correct answer. The web shop can use several ways of storing your search history and history of the products you have visited. For example, the web shop can use cookies stored on your computer, a history linked to your account (in case you are logged in), and a history linked to the IP address you are using. Option A is the only likely answer of the possibilities to choose from.

19. Multi-factor authentication can be an effective security measure. Which of the following is an example?
    A. Asking two passwords
    B. **Logging in on specific mainframes (correct)**
    C. Fingerprint authentication
    D. Iris scan

Info:

B is the correct answer. If you need to log in on a specific mainframe computer (using your password), one factor used to authenticate is the specific mainframe computer and the other is the password used to log in. It is not explicitly mentioned in the question itself that a password is also required, so this you should have presumed. Option A is the same factor used twice, and options C and D are just one factor.

20. A company in China wants to process personal data from EU data subjects. Which of the following is possibly the case?
    A. An adequacy decision is required for China
    B. If the data subjects were not targeted, the GDPR rules do not have to be followed (correct)
    C. China will have to first implement a new law
    D. Processing personal data in China will never be allowed

Info:

B is the correct answer. If the data subjects were, for example, visiting China, it is likely that personal data is collected. This personal data probably doesn't fall within the scope of the GDPR.

21. You are applying for a job in the same organization you worked for fifteen years ago. The company rejects your application based on your last performance appraisal it has on file from fifteen years ago. Which of the following is most likely applicable?
    A. The company can keep the performance appraisal because the lawful processing criterion legitimate interest is applicable
    B. The only way the company would have been allowed to keep the performance appraisal for fifteen years is valid consent (correct)
    C. An organization can keep performance appraisals as long as it wants because it is its own creation
    D. The applicant is not allowed to see the performance appraisal

Info:

B is the correct answer. It is unreasonable to consider any of the lawful processing criteria to be applicable fifteen years for keeping a performance appraisal of an employee that no longer works for the organization. Therefore, consent is the only possibility if indeed given for such a long period. This is misleading, as consent is problematic in an employer/employee relationship, but if the consent is provided after employment (for whatever reason), it is a possibility.

This information can be used for the following four questions:

Unexpectedly, you receive the news that you won a prize in a raffle. You do not remember having signed up for the raffle, so you investigate.

It turns out the online retailer where you purchased a sweater five years ago, has entered your e-mail address in the raffle. Your positive surprise turns into amazement at the retailer's audacity.

The next day you decide to send an access request since you want to know what exactly the retailer still processes. You receive a negative response, claiming the retailer opted to delete your personal data instead.

22. In order to keep your e-mail address for as long as the retailer has, which of the following is required?
    A. Legitimate interest
    B. A retroactive contract
    C. A valid lawful processing criterion (correct)
    D. A data protection impact assessment

Info:
C is the correct answer. The answer is quite general but therefore fits (unlike answer A, which is not necessarily applicable). B is clearly incorrect, and D is not necessarily required.

23. The retailer deleted your personal data. Which of the following is likely applicable?
   A. The retailer should have requested the data protection authority's advice
   B. The retailer was not allowed to delete your personal data when you requested it (correct)
   C. The retailer should have requested the data protection authority's permission
   D. The retailer has a legitimate interest in keeping the inner workings of his business confidential, hence the deletion is justified

Info:

B is the correct answer. When you request a copy of your personal data from a controller, the controller will have to provide the personal data it processes at that moment. Deleting the personal data is not a way to escape the obligation to provide a copy of the personal data.

24. If, apart from using the e-mail address for the raffle, the e-mail address is part of the invoice, which of the following lawful processing criteria is likely applicable?
   A. Required to comply with a legal obligation (correct)
   B. Necessary for the performance of a contract
   C. Legitimate interest of the data subject
   D. Legitimate interest of the controller

Info:

A is the correct answer. On invoices there likely is a legal requirement to have them available as required by certain fiscal laws. You could also argue it is necessary for the performance of a contract, such as the warranty on the item purchased, but in that case, it is unlikely that the e-mail address is only present on the invoice (therefore no need for the invoice specifically on the side of the controller).

25. What did the online retailer have to do at the very least before entering your e-mail address in the raffle?
    A. Increase security
    B. Update the privacy notice, and send it to you (correct)
    C. Migrate to a cloud-based solution
    D. Perform a data protection impact assessment

Info:

B is the correct answer. A controller needs to inform the data subject on how it processes the data subject's personal data. Of the options to choose from, this means that updating the privacy notice is required (at least).

26. Sensitive personal data is covered under Article 9 of the GDPR. How can sensitive personal data best be described?
    A. Personal data that is manifestly made public
    B. Personal data that has been obtained by data mining a large number of transactions
    C. Personal data that generally requires a higher level of protection, and a condition to be met beyond Article 6 (correct)
    D. Personal data for which a data protection impact assessment is always required

Info:

C is the correct answer. Sensitive personal data has a definition, which includes several categories that can be found in Article 9 of the GDPR, but the reason C is the correct answer here is that it describes the extra protection required and extra condition to be met (consent in many cases).

27. You request your personal data from an organization, and find out your address is incorrect despite having updated it. Which of the following is likely the case?

A. The integrity principle has been compromised

B. The lawful processing criterion has become void

C. The organization will automatically receive a fine

D. The accuracy principle has not been respected (correct)

Info:

D is the correct answer. A controller should keep the personal data it processes as accurately as possible. Especially when the data subject has corrected the personal data in the past, since not using the updated personal data would practically be denying the data subject the right to correct its personal data (see Article 16 of the GDPR, the right to rectification).

28. Which of the following would likely not be considered an establishment in the EU or targeting EU citizens?

A. An online retailer based in the US, selling printed flags on demand, including those of EU member states (correct)

B. A Canadian online retailer allowing for payment in Croatian currency

C. An online retailer based in Greece, focusing on the US market

D. A local grocery store on the border with the EU, selling EU products cheaper, using price tags in the language of the EU country it borders with

Info:

A is the correct answer. There is nothing in option A that indicates that the US organization is targeting data subjects in the EU. Therefore, since it is not based in the EU, nor processing in the EU, and is not targeting EU citizens, it is outside the scope of the GDPR.

29. An online retailer where you have complained in the past still has a record of your complaints. Where would you have expected to be informed about this practice?
    A. In the privacy notice, before sending a complaint
    B. In the sales contract, at the time of ordering
    C. On the website of the retailer, after submitting the order form
    D. In the privacy notice, before placing an order (correct)

Info:

D is the correct answer. Perhaps a lawful processing criterion applies for keeping complaints, but a data subject should be informed on how his/her personal data will be processed.

30. Organizations do not always respect the principle of purpose limitation. Of the following, which is an example?
    A. Storing the gathered personal data in several systems, including on a backup
    B. Processing personal data in several affiliates of the organization
    C. Placing an e-mail address, gathered in the context of a sale, on a mailing list (correct)
    D. Storing information about the processing in the data processing inventory

Info:

C is the correct answer. An e-mail address used for a sale should only be used for that sale (and perhaps for any legal requirements, such as storing the invoice with the e-mail address on it). When the e-mail address is collected for one thing (the sale), and then used for something not in line with that purpose (the mailing list), the purpose limitation principle is not respected. Mailing lists are tricky, and are allowed with an opt-out, but the opt-out is not mentioned anywhere (the question is somewhat misleading because you have to assume that you shouldn't assume the opt-out possibility was not provided).

31. Which of the following least likely requires a data processing agreement?
    A. **An accountancy firm handling your business' taxes (correct)**
    B. A cloud provider, hosting your organization's backup
    C. An organization, processing publicly available social media data your organization has mined
    D. A bakery, sending your employees a Christmas bread

Info:

A is the correct answer. A business' tax information does not necessarily contain personal data. Even if it could include personal data, it is not clear it concerns a controller/processor relationship. For all the other options to choose from, it is quite clear that a processor processing personal data is involved. The cloud provider (processor) is hosting (processing) an organization's (controller) backup (which more likely than not contains personal data). Social media data is personal data, regardless of it being publicly available, and thus requires a data processing agreement. The bakery needs to process the addresses of your employees in order to send them the Christmas bread (thus you are the controller, the bakery the processor, and your employees the data subjects).

32. The data protection authority needs to be notified in certain cases. Of the following, which is least likely a data breach?
    A. An e-mail sent to the wrong addressee
    B. An external hard drive that was lost
    C. **Processing that was not mentioned in the privacy notice (correct)**
    D. A stolen laptop

Info:

C is the correct answer. Processing not included in the privacy notice is not allowed, but not necessarily a data breach (if the controller does it consciously, for example).

33. The term "appropriate technical and organizational measures" can seem like a vague concept. Which of the following best describes this concept?
    A. A privacy policy adopted to the financial means allocated by the CEO
    B. Full encryption on backups
    C. Role-based access control
    D. A context-dependent level of security measures (correct)

Info:

D is the correct answer. The term appropriate indicates it depends on the context, which in this instance means balancing between the risks and available security measures (you don't always need the maximum level of protection).

34. Awareness within an organization is created least effectively with which of the following?
    A. A privacy policy of the organization
    B. Employee training for a large part of the staff
    C. A security policy
    D. A privacy notice on the website (correct)

Info:

D is the correct answer. A privacy notice generally tends to have an informational character. The other options have more of an instructional character. Therefore, since awareness is most likely created with instruction, D is the correct answer. Here you have to assume that "awareness" refers to how to deal with personal data, which makes sense given that A, B, and C pertain to this and option D does not.

35. Of the following, which person is least desirable to sign a data processing agreement on the controller side?
   A. The CIO
   B. The data protection officer (correct)
   C. The CEO
   D. The procurement manager

Info:

B is the correct answer. The data protection officer is supposed to be independent. If the data protection officer is not independent, there is a (potential) conflict of interest between the task of monitoring the organization's compliance and the financial/business interests of the organization. A data protection officer should thus not sign anything as a representative of the organization.

36. A data breach notification can be required in case of a data breach. Who in an organization is responsible for the data breach notification being sent?
   A. The CISO
   B. The data protection officer
   C. The privacy officer
   D. The CEO (correct)

Info:

D is the correct answer. The CEO is the highest level of management, which is ultimately responsible. This does not mean the CEO personally sends out the data breach notifications, but the CEO is responsible for it being sent out.

37. For which of the following is consent least likely required?
   A. Data pertaining to children
   B. Sensitive financial data, regarding bankruptcy (correct)
   C. Fingerprints
   D. Observable biometric data

Info:

B is the correct answer. Financial data is not a category of personal data that falls under Article 9 of the GDPR and is, therefore, least likely to require consent. For personal data of children, the parents need to consent, and fingerprints and observable biometric data are both biometric data and fall under Article 9 of the GDPR. There are ways of reasoning that lead to the sensitive financial data being the most likely option to require consent, but nothing in the phrasing of the question suggests that an exception applies to the requirement of consent for options A, C, and D.

38. In which of the following was the European Economic Area established?
   A. The Agreement on the European Economic Area (correct)
   B. The treaty of Lisbon
   C. The treaty of Vienna
   D. The treaty of Milan

Info:

A is the correct answer. The other treaties are thrown in there to mislead you. On the exam, you might be thrown off by how obvious the answer is, so learn how to deal with your nerves in such situations.

39. It is not always clear whether something can indirectly lead to uncovering new personal data. Which of the following will most likely lead to the unintended uncovering of sensitive personal data?

    A. The loss of a credit card, found by wrongdoers
    B. Malware, uncovering all technical aspects of your computer
    C. A strike, where members of a union decide to collectively go on strike (correct)
    D. An online survey, without open-text fields

Info:

C is the correct answer. Assume here that it is clear to the observers that when they see the employees on strike they make the link to the union, and trade union membership falls under Article 9 of the GDPR, and the employer can clearly link the missing employees to that union because of the strike. Another aspect here is the unintended character, since options A, B, and D pertain to the intended uncovering of personal data.

40. Prior to the GDPR, there was the Data Protection Directive. Which of the following is generally not a difference between a Directive and a Regulation?

    A. Regulations require member states to implement its requirements but leave more freedom than a Directive (correct)
    B. Fewer requirements of a Regulation are open to a different extent of implementation
    C. Directives lay aims for the member states, Regulations are applied in their entirety
    D. A Directive needs to be implemented into law, whereas a regulation does not

Info:

A is the correct answer. The opposite is the case because Directives leave more freedom in this regard.

41. A processor has purchased a new type of security software after starting to work for a new client. What is this likely the direct result of?
    A. A GDPR requirement
    B. A condition in the privacy notice
    C. The processor's privacy policy
    D. A clause in the data processing agreement (correct)

Info:

D is the correct answer. The data processing agreement will have requirements regarding the level of security (although perhaps not necessarily specifying the security software). Thus, it is possible that this requirement triggered the processor to purchase the new security software to ensure reaching the level of security agreed on in the data processing agreement. It is not required by the GDPR or privacy notice (although the level of security does flow out of this, applicable to the controller), and if it were due to the processor's privacy policy then the security software would have been purchased before taking on the new client.

42. One of the lawful processing criteria is "necessary for the performance of a contract". What best describes this?
    A. An address is always needed to complete a contract, which can be considered personal data
    B. The details specified in the contract regarding all the data subject's part of the processing
    C. A piece of information from the data subject, without which it can reasonably be expected that part of the contract cannot be completed (correct)
    D. A contract specifying appropriate technical and organizational measures for processing

Info:

C is the correct answer. The data subject needs to be part of the contract, the personal data needs to be relevant for the performance of the contract, and the lawful processing criterion is no longer applicable once the contract has been completed.

43. Social media organizations can make web beacons available. Of the following, which best describes the likely process?
    A. The user agrees to a transparent process of tracking all over the web
    B. A tracking cookie is installed, uploading the full browser history to the social media organization for advertisement purposes
    C. Once the user clicks on the web beacon, it registers the visit to the social media organization
    D. **A transparent pixel is placed on any website, and when that website is visited, that visit is registered by the social media organization (correct)**

Info:

D is the correct answer. See the earlier explanations of web beacons/tracking pixels. It is placed on a website (linked to, as it were), then loaded from the third party's server (social media organization), and therefore the social media organization sees which IP address loaded the pixel (and can link the visit to that specific website to their users with the same IP address).

44. In the past, many employers monitored their employees' online behavior. If, nowadays, an employer has access to its employees' browser history, what is likely required?
    A. A bring your own device policy
    B. A secure server for storing user data
    C. A data protection impact assessment
    D. **A valid lawful processing criterion and a privacy notice (correct)**

Info:

D is the correct answer. This is a tricky yet easy answer. A valid (applicable) lawful processing criterion is always required. Options B and C seem to address the sensitivity of the situation but are not necessarily required, and are added to mislead the reader.

45. When placing CCTV cameras in a building, which of the following is likely the least important consideration?
    A. **When the camera is pointed at the entrance, it could reveal the late arrival of employees (correct)**
    B. When the camera is pointed at a hallway containing restroom doors, it could reveal sensitive personal data
    C. When the camera is pointed at someone's desk, this could be disproportionate
    D. The retention of the recordings could require a strict policy

Info:
A is the correct answer. Not only is the arrival time likely already revealed by other means (like scanning a badge), it is also the least important of the options provided. Be careful with where you install CCTV though because as option B is trying to illustrate, an illness that requires frequent visits to the bathroom could be revealed this way.

46. When claiming damages from a violation of the GDPR, what is required?
    A. A mental breakdown due to the complicatedness of a privacy notice
    B. **To be able to show a form of damage as a consequence of a violation of the GDPR (correct)**
    C. The stress caused after finding out what exactly an organization knows/processes
    D. The result of a data protection authority investigation needs to be present in court, to prove damages

Info:
B is the correct answer. You cannot claim what you cannot prove. This is not an explicit requirement of the GDPR, so it requires you to reason to this answer. Options A and C are too specific here. Option D is not required.

47. Data protection officers have a special place in an organization. Of the following, which is least likely true?
  A. **The data protection officer is the highest level of management in the organization (correct)**
  B. The CEO can overrule the data protection officer
  C. The data protection officer is not required to be part of the data protection impact assessment team
  D. A data protection officer is never mandatory

Info:

A is the correct answer. The data protection officer is supposed to be independent, and therefore cannot be in a management position. The data protection officer does report to the highest level of management.

48. Regarding the right to be forgotten, which of the following is true?
  A. **An organization does not necessarily have to stop processing your personal data (correct)**
  B. An organization is always required to request extensive identification
  C. The personal data is not required to be deleted from low-risk backups
  D. The data protection officer is responsible for the deletion

Info:

A is the correct answer. If there is, for example, a legal requirement for the controller to keep the personal data (such as an invoice required by tax laws), the controller can keep processing (part of) the personal data.

49. Sometimes the data subjects need to be notified of a data breach. In which of the following is a notification least likely required?
   A. **The leak of a large list of partially masked IP addresses of a certain website (correct)**
   B. A misaddressed e-mail, containing a message regarding the dietary preferences of several people
   C. A list of students' grades being posted online publicly, contrary to university policy
   D. A backup server running without password protection for a few days

Info:

A is the correct answer. When the IP addresses are partially masked they are likely not considered personal data (unless the masked IP address is unique). In addition, an IP address by itself is not revealing. So, if nothing is linked to the IP address (such as the websites visited by that IP address), there are no significant consequences for the data subject.

50. Students hack into their political science professor's computer and steal the exam before exam day. Which of the following is most likely true?
    A. The professor intended to publish the exam, therefore it can be considered manifestly made public
    B. If the exam composed by the professor contains the professor's political views, the exam should be considered sensitive personal data (correct)
    C. As soon as the professor finds out, the data subjects are required to be informed
    D. The professor can claim damages from the university based on Article 82 of the GDPR

Info:

B is the correct answer. Article 9 of the GDPR describes political opinions as being sensitive personal data. Therefore, the exam contains sensitive personal data. If the question went further and asked about whether consent was required, then this would be the case until the exam was published by the professor (which can be seen as manifestly made public).

51. Personal data can be made anonymous or pseudonymous. Which if the following is not correct?
    A. No protection is required for anonymous data
    B. Strict protection can be required for pseudonymous data
    C. A separate set of information can be used to reverse pseudonymous data
    D. They are both reversible (correct)

Info:

D is the correct answer. Although personal data that is made pseudonymous means that an identifier is assigned to the elements of the data. For example, a list of names with the height and weight. If the names are replaced with numbers, for example as a security measure in case the data leaks, can be reversed if there is a list with which number belongs to which name. In this case, the data is pseudonymized. If the names were permanently deleted (and there is no other way of identifying anyone in the list), then the data would be anonymous, which is irreversible per definition.

52. You download a list of names and occupations from a website. After you replace the names with numbers, which of the following is most likely true?
   A. The new list no longer contains personal data
   B. The new list contains anonymous data
   C. The new list contains pseudonymous data (correct)
   D. The public data was never personal data

Info:
C is the correct answer. The data is pseudonymized since the source website still contains the information and this makes the process reversible. If the information were not available on the website (or anywhere else), the list could qualify as anonymous data.

53. If a controller intends to keep personal data for a longer period than needed, which data processing principle is likely not respected?
   A. Storage limitation (correct)
   B. Proportionality
   C. Accuracy
   D. Integrity

Info:
A is the correct answer. The storage limitation principle pertains to keeping data no longer than necessary. This is a clear description of a violation of the storage limitation principle. The proportionality principle is perhaps also violated, as it is disproportional to keep the personal data longer than necessary, but primarily the storage limitation principle is violated. Both A and B are correct, but A is more clearly correct and therefore the answer you should select.

54. If a processor wants to use personal data it initially collected for a controller for its own purposes, which data protection principle is likely not respected?
    A. Proportionality
    B. Storage limitation
    C. Accuracy
    D. Purpose limitation (correct)
Info:

D is the correct answer. A processor which collects personal data for a controller collects that data for the purpose to which the lawful processing criterion the controller relies on is applicable. Therefore, whatever the processor does with the personal data beyond the instructions of the controller, is not in line with the purpose. Hence, the purpose limitation principle is not respected.

55. Which lawful processing criterion requires a controller to do the most analysis?
    A. Contractual necessity
    B. Consent
    C. Legal obligation
    D. Legitimate interest (correct)
Info:

D is the correct answer. Legitimate interest requires a balancing of the interests of the controller and the data subject(s), and therefore can be considered to require analysis. For the other lawful processing criteria, it should be clearer whether it is applicable or not.

56. Of the following, which is not a condition for consent?
    A. Freely given
    B. Written (correct)
    C. Specific
    D. Reversible

Info:

B is the correct answer. Consent does not have to be written. A controller does have to prove that the data subject provided consent, but this can be registered in different ways (such as an audio recording in case of consent over the phone).

57. A controller has obtained consent for placing a customer on a mailing list after a sale. The data subject then notifies the controller he/she no longer consents. What does the controller need to do?
    A. Delete all personal data of the data subject
    B. Provide a copy of all personal data to the data subject
    C. Update the privacy notice
    D. Stop processing the personal data for the mailing list (correct)

Info:

D is the correct answer. Consent is only valid if it is reversible. Therefore, when the data subject objects after having given consent, the processing needs to stop from that moment onwards (of course reasonable practical limitations need to be taken into account, but perhaps this will not be on your exam).

58. Regarding informing data subjects about third parties, which of the following is not true?
   A. It needs to be explicit that third parties are involved
   B. Data subjects need to be informed about third parties before the processing starts
   C. **The names of the third parties need to be mentioned (correct)**
   D. Third parties outside of the EU might require additional measures

Info:

C is the correct answer. Article 13 (e) of the GDPR mentions "recipients or categories of recipients", meaning it is also acceptable to only mention the categories of recipients.

59. Trolling bots are actively bothering people on social media websites. What are these trolling bots possibly?
   A. Internet of things
   B. Malware
   C. Script kiddies
   D. **Artificial intelligence (correct)**

Info:

D is the correct answer. From the description it appears these trolling bots appear to be operating somewhat autonomously. The autonomous working of the trolling bots fits the definition of artificial intelligence (although perhaps not perfectly). Perhaps you have not come across the term trolling bots, but you can likely use the same reasoning with the term "bots".

60. Of the following, which is the least comprehensive law?
    A. **CAN-SPAM (correct)**
    B. POPI
    C. PIPEDA
    D. GDPR

Info:

A is the correct answer. You do not need to have in-depth knowledge of these, but you do require to know the names of these laws and a general description. From this general information, you should know that the GDPR, PIPEDA, and POPI are somewhat similar in scope. CAN-SPAM is limited in scope, and therefore least comprehensive.

61. Of the following, which is an example of self-regulation?
    A. **PCI-DS (correct)**
    B. A directive
    C. A regulation
    D. A member state's national law

Info:

A is the correct answer. This is the Payment Card Industry Data Security Standard, which is an initiative of the payment card industry. Therefore, it is self-regulation, as the industry creates standards to regulate itself.

62. Everyone's online presence leaves a mark. What is it called when advertisers seek you out because of this?
    A. Social media advertising
    B. Cookie analysis
    C. **Online behavioral advertising (correct)**
    D. Online tracking

Info:

C is the correct answer. The name gives the answer away, as it involves advertising. Social media advertising can be a form of online behavioral advertising, but this does not necessarily have to be the case. Online tracking and cookie analysis precede the advertiser selecting you, so therefore C is the best answer.

63. An organization refuses to issue company phones, yet
requires employees to own a phone to make emergency
phone calls. What can this likely be called?
  A. Illegitimate processing
  B. Legitimate interest
  C. Consent not freely given
  D. Bring your own device (correct)

Info:

D is the correct answer. The practice of employees bringing their
own device is called "bring your own device". It is not necessarily
illegitimate processing, since it is not clear whether processing of
personal data actually takes place.

64. Spreadsheet applications do not have to be loaded from a
user's hard drive, but can also be loaded from an external
server. What can this be called?
  A. A cloud server
  B. Software as a service (correct)
  C. An encrypted connection
  D. External data processing

Info:

B is the correct answer. Think of some of the latest applications
available in most offices. The latest version is loaded from (and runs
on) different computers, which is called software as a service. D also
sounds correct but is not as specific as B.

65. How can you best describe the role of the European Data Protection Board?
    A. Litigate
    B. Investigate
    C. Legislate
    D. Guide (correct)

Info:

D is the correct answer. The EDPB can provide guidance. It does not litigate, perform investigations, or create legislation. The EDPB is composed of representatives of the data protection authorities of the member states. These data protection authorities perform the investigations (for which they can collaborate), and the EDPB does not perform investigations.

66. Employees need to know how management intends to translate data protection requirements into action. Where will the staff most likely find this information?
    A. The GDPR
    B. Procedures (correct)
    C. The organization's privacy notice
    D. Advice from the data protection officer

Info:

B is the correct answer. Procedures are the documents (generally) that contain the instructions for the employees. It is thus the most likely source for the information on how the organization implements regulatory requirements. The data protection officer's advice is only advice, and cannot be seen as an instruction or an approach of the organization (management can decide to ignore the advice, for example).

67. There are multiple ways of safeguarding personal data in international data processing. For processing EU personal data by a processor in an adequate country, which of the following is needed?
   A. Nothing, as the country is adequate
   B. A data processing agreement (correct)
   C. Binding corporate rules and a data processing agreement
   D. Binding corporate rules

Info:

B is the correct answer. A data processing agreement is always needed when a processor is involved. Relying on binding corporate rules is not possible, since a processor is a third party, and binding corporate rules can only pertain to the processing of personal data within the same organization (present in different countries).

68. Data processors can be required to cooperate with the data protection authority's investigation in case of a data breach. In case the processor does not cooperate due to a clause missing in the data processing agreement, who is responsible?
   A. The processor has its own responsibility, based on the GDPR
   B. The responsibility for data breaches is agreed on in the data processing agreement
   C. The controller is responsible for ensuring the processing is done safely (correct)
   D. The data subject is informed in the privacy notice if the controller distances itself from responsibility for data breaches

Info:

C is the correct answer. It is safe to always choose the answer that implies the controller is responsible. The processor is responsible to comply with the investigation, but the controller is still responsible. Option A appears to be correct, but it does not address the question to the extent option C addresses the question (when in doubt, always assess whether an answer that seems correct addresses the question completely).

69. How can the European Data Protection Supervisor best be described?

   A. The data protection authority of the institutions of the EU (correct)
   B. Representing the member states' data protection authorities
   C. The EU data protection authorities' coordination body
   D. The only authority to impose fines

Info:

A is the correct answer. You will not need to know much about the European Data Protection Supervisor, other than that it is the data protection authority that monitors the EU institutions (to which a regulation different from the GDPR applies).

70. Privacy by design has become a requirement in the GDPR. Which of the following best describes privacy by design?

   A. A method/principle to embed privacy in the product/processing (correct)
   B. A way to turn off all tracking and stay anonymous
   C. Required program settings, so you can opt-out of any processing of personal data
   D. Compatibility with privacy-protecting browser settings

Info:

A is the correct answer. Options B, C, and D are examples rather than a description. In addition, these examples do not fully cover privacy by design.

71. Where does privacy by design start?
    A. At the layout design phase
    B. At the testing phase
    C. As early as possible (correct)
    D. At the data protection officer's approval

Info:

C is the correct answer. The key is that privacy is included in the design, and to ensure this the best answer here is C. Option A might throw you off because it contains the word "design", but it is not correct since it is quite specific and whether this would ensure that privacy is taken into account in the entire design is left out (design of other things than the layout could have preceded it, for example).

72. You are an employee of one of the institutions of the EU. You audit the European Commission. Which institution are you most likely working for?
    A. The parliament
    B. The European Court of Auditors (correct)
    C. The European External Action Service
    D. The Council of Europe

Info:

B is the correct answer. The European Court of Auditors is auditing the institutions of the EU, and the European Commission is one of the institutes of the EU.

73. A data protection impact assessment can be mandatory for certain processing. Which of the following best describes the outcome of a data protection impact assessment?
    A. A security standard for risky processing
    B. A way for the data protection officer to communicate his/her opinion
    C. A collaborative document from both management and the data protection officer
    D. **An inventory of risks and mitigative measures (correct)**

Info:

D is the correct answer. All of the options can be present after a data protection impact assessment since the assessment may show that these measures are needed. However, option D is the direct result of the data protection impact assessment.

74. Multinational organizations will have to fall under a data protection authority. Under which data protection authority will a multinational organization likely fall?
    A. The trans-EU data protection authority
    B. The local ombudsman
    C. The ambassador's data protection authority
    D. **The data protection authority of the country of its head office in the EU (correct)**

Info:

D is the correct answer. Options A, B, and C are incorrect. The data protection authority of the EU member state that hosts the European (head) office of a multinational is likely the data protection authority for that multinational organization.

75. In case an employee is new to an organization and receives an access request, what is the best place to start?
    A. **A data processing inventory (correct)**
    B. Data protection impact assessments
    C. The privacy policy
    D. The organization's cloud backup

Info:

A is the correct answer. The data processing inventory (records of processing) should provide an overview of which personal data is being processed, and in which processes. Thus, by looking at the data processing inventory it should be clear where the personal data that needs to be provided for the access request can be found.

76. An organization's management does not always welcome the advice of the data protection officer. What can management do when it disagrees with the data protection officer?
    A. Move the person who is the data protection officer to a different role
    B. Perform a data protection impact assessment with a different team in order to get a different outcome
    C. **Continue with the planned processing regardless (correct)**
    D. Leave the processing out of the data processing inventory

Info:

C is the correct answer. Management is not bound by the advice of the data protection officer and therefore may opt to ignore it and continue with whatever the data protection officer advised against. However, management is responsible for the compliance of the organization, so if the data protection officer's advice would have protected them against incompliance, it is unwise to act contrary to the data protection officer's advice.

77. The EU consists of institutions and bodies. Which of the following is not one of the EU's institutions?
    A. European Central Bank
    B. Council of the EU
    C. European Commission
    D. Council of Europe (correct)

Info:
D is the correct answer. The Council of Europe is an organization to uphold human rights, democracy, and the rule of law in Europe. It has 47 member states and is not an institution of the EU.

78. Processors at times hire third parties to process for them. If that processor hires another third party to process on behalf of them, what is that third party called?
    A. A third-party responsible
    B. A controller
    C. A processor (correct)
    D. A sub-controller

Info:
C is the correct answer. A processor hired by a processor is also called a processor (or sub-processor).

This information can be used for the following four questions:

A mental health coaching firm has recently started conducting its activities online. Not only can clients book in-person appointments, but coaching sessions can also take place through an internet connection, from the comfort of the client's home.

Clients are requested to download a video calling application, either on their phone or on their computer. The application was chosen by the organization, as it is the only application compatible with its hardware.

Not all clients are comfortable in front of the camera. Unfortunately, the application does not have the option to disable the video stream. Because of this, several clients have pointed the camera away from them.

For clients, the software is free to use, but the coaching firm pays a subscription for a certain number of consecutive calls at a time. Practically this means one license per coach.

79. Given that the video cannot be disabled by the client, what is most clearly not respected?
    A. Transparency
    B. Privacy notice
    C. Privacy by design (correct)
    D. Specific consent

Info:
C is the correct answer. When an option is not available that would have enhanced privacy, it can be concluded that privacy by design has likely not been applied to the correct extent (regardless of whether there is a lawful processing criterion for the video).

80. Since the coaching firm chose the video software, what is the company that sells/hosts/maintains the software?
    A. A controller
    B. A processor (correct)
    C. An external partner
    D. A co-responsible

Info:

B is the correct answer. The coaching firm chose and thus determined the means and purposes, and the seller/host/maintenance organization (processor) therefore processes on behalf of the coaching firm (controller).

81. Based on the nature of the activities of the coaching company, combined with the new video calling practice, which of the following would you consider the biggest risk?
    A. The data processing agreement does not contain a clause about sub-processors
    B. No approval for the new method has been provided by the data protection officer
    C. A data breach is likely to occur when clients record the sessions
    D. Sensitive personal data is processed without adequate technical and organizational measures (correct)

Info:

D is the correct answer. It concerns mental health, so this is sensitive personal data. If privacy by design is already so poorly applied in the development of the software, this risk is quite likely.

82. Regarding the video stream the coaches use, what is the most likely applicable lawful processing criterion?
    A. **Legitimate interest, provided that clients are able to turn their camera away (correct)**
    B. Contract, as the clients have a contract with the coaching firm
    C. Vital interest, since the coaching can concern mental issues
    D. Consent, because the processing cannot commence without consent

Info:

A is the correct answer. The video service itself is not necessary, since the coaching can also be done by phone or in-person. Therefore, the contract and vital interest criteria don't apply. Legitimate interest seems appropriate here, as the option to turn away the camera weighs positively on the balance of interests. It is not a 100% clear answer, but from the available options, A is the most likely answer.

This information can be used for the following five questions:

You build and host websites. The content of these websites is dictated by your customers. Your customers range from individuals with hobby websites to small business owners' websites.

The websites can be simple and purely informational, or complex and significantly interactive. This leads to visitors loading information only, or loading and leaving information.

Recently, more and more customers are requesting you to sign a contract detailing the security and reporting requirements. This is a big hassle, and in order to reduce your workload, you ask your customers to sign a standard contract you composed yourself.

83. What is the contract referred to above called?
    A. A sub-processor contract
    B. A data protection impact assessment
    C. A data transfer agreement
    D. A data processing agreement (correct)

Info:
D is the correct answer. Security and reporting requirements are usually included in a data processing agreement. It could also be included in a data transfer agreement, but since you are a processor in this case it is not a transfer agreement but a data processing agreement.

84. What would you call the visitor of a website in case the visit is interactive?
   A. A processor
   B. A data subject (correct)
   C. A co-controller
   D. A sub-processor

Info:

B is the correct answer. Personal data of the visitor is likely collected through the interactive nature of the website (think about the registration of choices made, for example). Therefore, the visitor becomes a data subject. In addition, the other options are incorrect since the visitor likely does not process any personal data (although far-fetched examples could be produced here that indicate the contrary).

85. One of your customers instructs you to place a transparent pixel on sections of its website, in order to log which IP address opened which section at which time. What is this pixel called?
   A. A tracking frame
   B. A pixel query
   C. A web beacon (correct)
   D. An analytical cookie

Info:

C is the correct answer. This is called a web beacon (or tracking pixel). Even if it is not from a third party (like a social media website) it is still a web beacon.

86. In the case of the transparent pixel, which principle is likely violated when logging these details?
    A. Transparency
    B. Accuracy
    C. Integrity and confidentiality
    D. Proportionality (correct)

Info:

D is the correct answer. The details on who visits what at what time are likely unnecessary for the purpose for which the data subject visits the website. Therefore, it can be said to not be proportional.

87. In this case, when you hire a company to do part of the work for you because your clients are too demanding, what are you?
    A. A processor (correct)
    B. A controller
    C. A sub-processor
    D. A co-controller

Info:

A is the correct answer. Although it might appear to suggest a shift to becoming a controller, you were originally a processor and just because you hire another processor this does not change. You would only become a controller if you hire a processor for your own work, for example for work that does not relate to building the websites for your customers (such as tax services for your company).

88. In which of the following situations would binding corporate rules be most appropriate?

   A. An organization in the EU cooperating with a private organization in Canada, exchanging employee personal data

   B. A government organization using contractors in several countries outside of the EU

   C. An organization with affiliates in Germany and Bahrain, not exchanging sensitive personal data (correct)

   D. When using a processor in the US, assuming there is a suitable replacement for Privacy Shield

Info:

C is the correct answer. Binding corporate rules can substitute standard contractual clauses and other mechanisms for the processing of personal data outside of the EU (but within the same organization). These binding corporate rules will need to be composed in a way that they ensure compliance with the GDPR, resulting in the part of the organization in Bahrain that is also bound by them to therefore process in accordance with the GDPR as a result.

89. Some processing of sensitive personal data is not restricted. Of the following, which is most likely restricted?
   A. Churches maintaining a member list of their members' religion
   B. **Employers processing union membership of their employees (correct)**
   C. A doctor processing medical data
   D. The processing of a national identification number by the tax services

Info:
A is the correct answer. Union membership falls under sensitive personal data as mentioned in Article 9 of the GDPR, and its processing is restricted. In this case, there is no apparent need for the employer to process the union membership. In addition, if consent were to be obtained it would possibly not be valid due to the possible pressure the employee experiences as he/she might fear consequences for the job (not freely given).

90. Which principle does role-based access control protect most?
   A. Storage limitation
   B. Proportionality
   C. Purpose limitation
   D. **Confidentiality (correct)**

Info:
D is the correct answer. Any method of access control is supposed to restrict access, hence keeping things more confidential.

Exam 3:

1. EEA stands for European Economic Area. Which of the following best describes the EEA?
   A. A data protection regulation
   B. An international agreement
   C. A data protection directive
   D. A set of EU member state rules

2. The European single market is sometimes referred to as the common market. Which countries are part of the European single market?
   A. The EU's member states, Iceland, Liechtenstein, and Norway
   B. The EU's member states
   C. The EU's member states and Canada
   D. The EU's member states and the US through Privacy Shield

3. European laws go through several institutions. Which institution drafts most laws?
   A. The European parliament
   B. The European council
   C. The European Commission
   D. The member states

4. There are many reasons for privacy protection. In a medical context, which of the following is the biggest benefit from increased medical privacy?
   A. Patients are more open during medical treatment
   B. The doctor can process insurance information faster
   C. Fines for violations of privacy
   D. Organizations are less likely to infringe on a person's privacy

5. A construction company puts up a billboard on its construction site, proudly announcing which celebrity will own the building. Which of the following is true?
   A. The construction company needs a valid lawful processing criterion to advertise this way
   B. Celebrity names are in the public domain, and therefore are not personal data
   C. Consent for this advertisement is implied in signing the construction contract
   D. If the advertising was based on consent, it need not be reversible, because of the significant cost of the billboard

6. Which court, also known as the Strasbourg court, judges cases beyond the EU regarding the European Convention of Human rights?
   A. The European Court of Justice
   B. The European Court of Human Rights
   C. The European Peace Court
   D. The Member states' national court

7. In 2006 the Data Retention Directive was passed. Under the Data Retention Directive, which of the following is correct?
   A. An e-mail must be stored for at least 24 months
   B. An IP address must be stored for at least six months
   C. Telecommunication is exempt from retention
   D. It was amended by the Directive on Privacy and Electronic Communications

8. Spam is a nuisance for many. Regarding the regulation of spam in the EU, where would you look?
   A. The e-privacy directive
   B. CAN-SPAM
   C. The Data Protection Directive
   D. The Data Retention Directive

9. You visit an anonymous support group. Attendants are asked to create a nickname. Which of the following is most likely true?
   A. If the nickname is linked to a phone number or e-mail address, it is personal data
   B. A nickname by itself can never constitute personal data
   C. A nickname by itself always constitutes personal data
   D. Use of the nickname requires consent

10. A data subject is the subject of personal data. Which of the following is least likely considered a data subject?
    A. The person that was the source for anonymous data
    B. An element of a data set
    C. The person part of a contract, not the one the lawful processing criterion "necessary for the performance of a contract"
    D. A person listed on a website

11. A controller determines the means and purposes of the processing. Which of the following is the best description of this?
    A. The final responsible for what happens to personal data processing-wise
    B. The designer of the security measures
    C. A party of the data processing agreement
    D. A party requesting another party to process personal data

12. The European Data Protection Board issues guidance from time to time. Which of the following is now required when using standard contractual clauses?
    A. A data protection impact assessment
    B. A data processing agreement
    C. A transfer impact assessment
    D. A privacy assessment

13. In a large organization, which department is most likely to order a privacy program?
    A. The privacy department
    B. The IT department
    C. The marketing department
    D. The compliance department

14. Which of the following is the least true regarding the right to object?
    A. After receipt of the request, the controller must act immediately
    B. The request to block processing for direct marketing is absolute
    C. Data subjects can object to processing for scientific research
    D. Data subjects can object to processing for the controller's legitimate interest

15. There are four defined classes of privacy. Which of the following is not one of them?
    A. Medical privacy
    B. Bodily privacy
    C. Territorial privacy
    D. Information privacy

16. The Justices of the Peace Act enacted in 1361 contained a certain level of privacy protection. How was this included?
    A. The army was forbidden to enter civilian houses
    B. Tax collectors were limited by law
    C. Churches were forbidden to keep records
    D. The arrest of peeping Toms

17. Which country implemented the first data protection law that took the potential of IT developments into account?
    A. Belgium
    B. Germany
    C. Austria
    D. The United States

18. There are many public sources for personal data. Which of the following is true for public personal data?
    A. Public personal data can be processed without restrictions
    B. Public personal data can be processed based on consent
    C. A controller never needs to provide a privacy notice for public personal data
    D. Processing of public personal data does not have to be recorded in the data processing inventory

19. A retailer has a wealth of data of its customers, all collected to complete the sales. What is true regarding further use of this data?
    A. The retailer can further process the data when only the elements are used that result in a sufficiently high level of data aggregation
    B. The retailer is free to sell the full data for research, as that is a legitimate interest
    C. The retailer would require consent to use anonymized data further, which would then lead to satisfying the lawful processing criterion
    D. The retailer would require a legal obligation to further process anonymous data

20. A company has a privacy policy on its website, for both guiding employees and informing data subjects. Which of the following is true?
    A. The privacy policy is likely too complicated to count as a privacy notice
    B. The employees don't require further information
    C. A privacy notice needs to be provided prior to processing
    D. The policy is likely suitable to convey the organization's attitude to personal data processing

21. A store collects phone IDs through Bluetooth scanning and tracks its customers as they move through the store. Which of the following is a danger?
    A. The employees that are aware of the practice won't be able to avoid being monitored
    B. The store can link the customer's purchases to the phone ID
    C. There is no way to capture the practice into a privacy notice
    D. Consent is required from the employees in order to use the practice

22. A shopping mall offers free WIFI. However, users need to consent to being tracked and provide their full names. Which of the following is most likely true?
    A. The controller requires the full name, otherwise, it cannot reverse the consent
    B. The consent is not valid, and the WIFI needs to be provided without consent or not at all
    C. The consent can be valid but depends on the retention period
    D. The shopping mall is free to collect the data it wants even without consent

23. A dating app sells the personal data it gathers. What is true about the privacy notice?
    A. This practice can reasonably be expected and needs no explicit mentioning
    B. It needs to clearly mention that your personal data is being sold, which personal data, and to whom
    C. Selling the personal data is required for the lawful processing criterion necessary for a contract
    D. A privacy notice is not necessary if the controller is based in the US

24. An international organization can opt to use Binding Corporate Rules for international transfers of personal data. Of the following, which least suffices as Binding Corporate Rules?
    A. A copy of the GDPR
    B. The internal security standards
    C. A privacy notice
    D. A Bring Your Own Device policy

This information can be used for the following five questions:

A service company maintains and operates a large campus where multiple companies are operating. It concerns a collection of factories and offices, fully surrounded by a fence. The property is owned by the service company.

The service company maintains all roads and buildings. Only the maintenance of one of the renter's plants is done by the company that built and operates the plant. The IT infrastructure is also maintained by the service company.

All users of the campus, at the individual employee level, are known to the service company. This is because of safety procedures, which legally require the service company to know who is present on-site. Everybody entering the site has a personal ID badge or a visitor badge linked to a copy of an identity card.

To improve safety, and address concerns regarding reckless behavior, the service company monitors all persons on the campus. This is done through CCTV, but the security staff also uses speeding cameras and issues a warning to the person linked to the license plate of the speeding vehicle.

25. In order to use CCTV, which of the following least likely needed to be done first?
    A. A data protection impact assessment
    B. Update the data processing inventory
    C. Adjust the privacy notice on the website
    D. Determine the appropriate retention period

26. In order to send a warning to the person linked to the license plate after a violation, which of the following lawful processing criteria is most likely applicable?
    A. Consent
    B. Vital interest
    C. Contract
    D. Legitimate interest

27. When linking a visitor badge to an individual, which of the following is most likely true?
    A. All relevant details can only be processed when consent is provided
    B. Making a copy of a person's ID card is unnecessary
    C. The person's national tax ID is sufficient
    D. A full copy of the ID card can be processed

28. Regarding the storage period of the information collected on the visitors, which of the following is most likely true?
    A. Storage can be based on backup retention periods
    B. Storage should be indefinite, as something can always be needed
    C. The retention period can be extended if another useful way of processing personal data comes up
    D. The storage period is linked to the lawful processing criterion

29. Which of the following of the service company's practices is not multi-factor authentication?
    A. Scanning a badge and showing an ID
    B. An account working only on a certain computer
    C. Scanning the badge and typing a passcode
    D. Checking if the shown ID belongs to the person showing it

30. An organization can improve data protection by implementing safeguards. Which is not a main type of safeguard?
    A. Administrative safeguard
    B. Detective safeguard
    C. Technical safeguard
    D. Physical safeguard

31. Which of the following are the information life cycle principles?
    A. Collection, Use, Disclosure, Storage, and Destruction
    B. Processing, Use, Disclosure, Storage, and Destruction
    C. Collection, Processing, Disclosure, Storage, and Destruction
    D. Collection, Processing, Retention, and Disclosure

32. There are several models of privacy protection. Which of the following is not a model of privacy protection?
    A. Comprehensive model
    B. Sectoral model
    C. Technical determinist model
    D. Co-regulatory model

33. Which of the following is least true regarding Binding Corporate Rules?
    A. The organization needs to be based in the EU
    B. They are legally binding
    C. It replaces data processing agreements
    D. The data protection authority can judge the Binding Corporate Rules to be inadequate

34. Which of the following is not a description of a risk?
    A. Threat x Vulnerability x Expected loss
    B. A negative occurrence
    C. The chance of a data breach
    D. The chance of a lost USB stick being accessed

35. Of the following, which is not a basic principle of role-based access control?
    A. Segregation of duties
    B. Least privilege
    C. Need to know or access
    D. Hierarchy approval

36. There are several ways of identifying someone through technology. How is it called when the settings of someone's browser are used to identify someone?
    A. Browser fingerprinting
    B. Technical identification
    C. A browser leak
    D. Phishing

37. The GDPR requires protection for certain types of data. Which of the following least likely requires protection?
    A. An organization's list of business-to-business contracts consisting of functional mailboxes
    B. An American tourist's personal data
    C. A mildly aggregated database with personal data
    D. A pseudonymized list of test subject data

38. Which of the following is least likely true regarding the relationship between a processor and a data subject?
    A. A processor is responsible for complying with a data access request
    B. The processor has a responsibility towards the data subject regarding secure processing of personal data
    C. The processor has no responsibility towards the data subject regarding the data processing agreement
    D. A data subject can ask a processor to provide the name of the controller

39. Which of the following is least likely true regarding sensitive personal data?
    A. A higher level of protection is required compared to that for non-sensitive personal data
    B. A different lawful processing criterion is needed than for personal data processed relying on legitimate interest
    C. Consent is the only possible lawful processing criterion
    D. There is a difference between the restrictions on newly generated sensitive personal data and public sensitive personal data

40. Which of the following requires the processing of personal data?
    A. Processing a list of highly aggregated data
    B. Publishing all third parties in the privacy notice
    C. Providing a privacy notice to a mailing list
    D. Formatting a cloud space

41. Of the following, which is least likely required for the completion of a contract to which the data subject is a party?
    A. A list of public data being processed at the request of a third-party
    B. The fulfillment of a retail order
    C. Being part of an employer's database
    D. Food delivery

42. The field of artificial intelligence has been making significant progress. Which of the following is least likely a privacy risk linked to artificial intelligence?
    A. New personal data is generated easily, by combining and analyzing data
    B. Consent is obtained in unclear ways, leading to overprocessing of personal data
    C. Personal data gets processed outside of the originally understood scope
    D. Encryption can prove less reliable as a security measure

This information can be used for the following four questions:

Recently you have been appointed the role of privacy officer at an international social media company. You work in a team with three other privacy officers, and you report to the CEO.

The social media company is not from the EU but has a website in almost every EU country, including the ability to translate text to the local language. No payments are required from users, but corporate pages cost money and can only be paid in US dollars.

Given how new the regulation is, you and your colleagues disagree on the interpretation from time to time. Whenever a disagreement arises, the CEO eventually chooses the most desirable interpretation. Although you notice that your colleagues' translation from law to practice often stems from your poor understanding of technology, the CIO often sides with them.

43. After another disagreement with your colleagues, your boss accuses you of not doing what is best for the company. Which of the following is true regarding disciplining a privacy officer?
    A. The GDPR provides protection against privacy officers being disciplined due to doing their job
    B. The company can discipline the privacy officer, as long as no labor laws are broken
    C. Only if the performance is bad, does the GDPR not restrict a change in role as a form of discipline
    D. An appraisal containing criticism on the privacy officer's social skills are intolerable in this context

44. From a privacy perspective, what can likely not be said about you reporting to the CIO?
    A. The CEO will be fully responsible for privacy
    B. The privacy officers will not be held responsible for decisions taken by management
    C. The CIO will be fully competent to make decisions regarding the allocation of budget
    D. The GDPR does not allow for the CIO to balance limited means between privacy and security

45. The social media company uses web beacons on other websites to see which of its users visit these websites. Which of the following is least likely true?
    A. This practice can be considered monitoring
    B. A data protection impact assessment is needed before starting the use of the web beacon
    C. There needs to be a proper balance between the invasiveness of the practice and the benefits it provides to the social media company and the users
    D. Data subjects do not need to be informed by the websites containing the web beacons

46. Given that the web beacon is also placed on sites of a political or sexual nature, what is likely the only lawful processing criterion that can be relied on?
    A. Legitimate interest
    B. Contract
    C. Consent
    D. Vital interest

47. An organization processes personal data, and during that processing, the legally required retention period gets longer. Which of the following is least likely true?
   A. The storage limitation is respected, despite the change in the retention period
   B. Given the extended retention period, the accuracy of the personal data is likelier to be negatively affected
   C. The data processing inventory will need to be updated
   D. Despite the longer retention period, the given consent remains valid

48. Which of the following is most likely true about the processing of sensitive personal data?
   A. Only information provided by the data subject can be considered sensitive personal data
   B. Consent is the only way to process sensitive personal data
   C. Only explicit information can reveal sensitive personal data
   D. Even if false, something can still be considered sensitive personal data

49. The EU institutions have their own regulation. On which lawful processing criterion can the EU institutions not rely?
   A. Consent
   B. Legitimate interest
   C. Legal obligation
   D. Public interest

50. When placing cookies, which of the following is most true?
    A. A privacy notice must be provided before placing any cookies
    B. If the user does not agree to the cookies, processing of personal data through cookies cannot take place and some services may not function
    C. For placing a third-party web beacon, the user can simply be referred to the third party after placing the web beacon
    D. No cookies are allowed without a lawful processing criterion

51. Which of the following is not a risk of not properly identifying a data subject for an access request?
    A. Unlawful processing
    B. Losing the original lawful processing criterion/criteria
    C. Someone other than the data subject sees the personal data
    D. A data breach

52. You rent a car and afterward find out that the rental agency placed you on a mailing list. What likely happened if this comes as a surprise?
    A. You were not shown a layered privacy notice
    B. No consent was obtained
    C. A data access request was not complied with
    D. You were not provided with the opportunity to opt-out

53. Cloud services are becoming more and more popular. Which of the following is an example of cloud computing?
    A. A web-based e-mail service
    B. Use of a modem
    C. Having mainframes connected
    D. Using a virtual private network

54. After renting a car, the rental agency sends you a fine because the car's GPS signaled that you crossed a national border (which costs extra). What could you have expected before?
    A. Information about GPS information being processed
    B. Information about paying fines
    C. The possibility to opt-out of receiving a fine
    D. A detailed list of third parties involved

55. An international organization in both the middle east and the EU has a set of internal guidelines on how to deal with processing personal data in a manner compliant with all applicable laws. What would this set of guidelines likely be called?
    A. A privacy notice
    B. A privacy policy
    C. Binding Corporate Rules
    D. Privacy Shield

56. Works councils can have an impact on the level of privacy in an organization. Of the following, where would a works council most likely have input?
    A. Updating the organization's privacy notice
    B. Installing CCTV cameras necessary for security
    C. Updating the organization's privacy policy
    D. Processing employee data using new payroll software

57. Of the following, what is the least likely lawful processing criterion to rely on as an employer processing personal data of employees?
    A. Legitimate interest
    B. Consent
    C. Contract
    D. Legal obligation

58. Some devices can be unlocked using a fingerprint. Which of the following complies most with the Privacy by Design principles?
    A. Making a connection with a secure server to verify the print
    B. Encrypting the print
    C. Using salting
    D. Storing the print on the device

59. Bring Your Own Device practices are becoming more and more popular. Which of the following best describes Bring Your Own Device?
    A. A situation where employees bring their own work laptop home to connect over a VPN
    B. Software to check corporate e-mail through a web browser
    C. CIO approval of the privacy policy
    D. Employees voluntarily using a private device to perform work tasks

60. There are several risks to take into account when implementing a whistleblowing program. Which of the following is the least likely risk?
    A. A wrongly addressed e-mail to the whistleblower
    B. Endangering the whistleblower by requiring disclosed of his/her identity
    C. Risking false data on a data subject when allowing anonymous whistleblowing
    D. Endangering those involved by not restricting access to the data sufficiently

61. Some companies perform a constant real-time check on what happens with the personal data they process. What can this be called?
    A. Surveillance
    B. Constant processing
    C. Data retention
    D. Monitoring

62. When processors and processors of processors (sub-processors) are involved, which of the following is most likely true?
    A. All processing parties that are not the controller will need to sign a data processing agreement
    B. When Binding Corporate Rules are in place, there is no need to sign a data processing agreement
    C. The controller is only responsible for the consequences of the actions of direct processors
    D. What needs to be signed depends on the country in which the processing takes place

63. When a government agency installs CCTV to monitor suspicious activity, which lawful processing criterion is least likely applicable?
    A. Consent
    B. Public task
    C. Legitimate interest
    D. Legal requirement

64. The GDPR introduced fines of as high as EUR 20 million or 4% of annual worldwide turnover. Which of the following is least likely going to result in a fine?
    A. A wrongfully addressed e-mail
    B. A systematic security flaw
    C. A wrongful processing
    D. A data breach due to negligence of management

65. An organization can audit its privacy practices. How can a privacy audit best be described?
    A. A check on the availability of data protection impact assessments where needed
    B. A thorough inspection of the data processing inventory
    C. A team appointed by the CIO verifying the security standards
    D. An independent assessment of the compliance with the relevant framework

66. When a processor collects personal data on behalf of a controller, which of the following is least likely true?
    A. The data subject needs to be shown a privacy notice
    B. The processor collects personal data beyond what is necessary for the purpose of the controller
    C. If the processor collects additional personal data for its own purposes, the controller is responsible
    D. The controller determines how the processor collects personal data, and thus needs a lawful processing criterion to be applicable

This information can be used for the following four questions:

A zoo has recently opened up a children's section where it allows kids to pet all the animals. Kids can be dropped off, and the parents can have some time for themselves. Every kid entering will receive a bracelet with a GPS to monitor where they are, so they will never get lost, and the parents can find their kids quickly.

As soon as a child enters the children's section, an actor in a crocodile suit will stand next to the child and a photo will be taken. The photo can later be purchased as a souvenir. Some children are shy, so the actor in the crocodile suit grabs their hands and positions them in front of the camera.

In addition to several supervisors, there are CCTV cameras throughout the zoo. The recordings are accessible for all staff employees, which is necessary because recordings are studied to figure out animal behavior.

67. Regarding the photograph taken of the child, which of the following is least likely true?
   A. A data access request should provide a copy of the photo taken
   B. The positioning of the children fits the legitimate interest in the zoo
   C. Consent from the parents would have to be obtained before taking the photo
   D. The zoo will need to choose a proportionate retention period for the photo taken

68. The data protection officer has some doubts regarding the level of access to the CCTV recordings. Which of the following is least likely true regarding this situation?
    A. The CEO will be responsible for taking the correct action
    B. If the data protection officer provides information to the CEO, there is no legal obligation to stop
    C. The organization does not have to provide the data protection officer permanent access to the CCTV recordings
    D. If found to be disproportionate, the data protection officer can restrict access to the CCTV recordings

69. The zoo has a privacy notice on its website, and the specifics are mentioned under all different activities. What can this likely be called?
    A. Privacy by Design
    B. Privacy by Default
    C. A just-in-time notice
    D. A layered privacy notice

70. The zoo owns an aquarium as well, located abroad, and named differently. In addition, the zoo uses a third party to manage the aquarium. Which of the following is most likely true if personal data is processed?
    A. For the zoo's aquarium, Binding Corporate Rules are sufficient, but with the third party a data processing agreement has to be signed
    B. Binding Corporate Rules are sufficient for any processing of personal data
    C. A data protection impact assessment is sufficient for any processing of personal data
    D. Nothing is required if the third party managing the aquarium is in a country that is deemed adequate

71. Passwords for websites are generally stored by making them unreadable for those who can assess them. What is this called?
    A. Hashing
    B. Salting
    C. A firewall
    D. Role-based access control

72. There are many ways in which an organization can be hijacked by hackers. Which of the following is the least direct cause of this?
    A. Installed malware
    B. A social engineering attack
    C. A database of stolen passwords
    D. An outdated virus scanner

73. Geolocation allows a controller to see where a data subject is or has been. Which of the following is least likely used to determine someone's location?
    A. IP address
    B. A web beacon
    C. GPS
    D. Multi-factor authentication

74. Not all countries have received an adequacy decision. Who/what/which of the following issues adequacy decisions?
    A. The European Commission
    B. The European Parliament
    C. The European Data Protection Authority
    D. The Member State authorities

75. Many people are bothered by the marketing practices of organizations. Which law would likely provide the biggest hindrance for controllers to send marketing to home addresses in the EU?
    A. The GDPR
    B. The e-privacy directive
    C. CAN-SPAM
    D. Directive 95

76. A controller can have a legal obligation to process certain personal data. Which of the following is the least likely source of such legal obligation?
    A. A customer requirement
    B. A financial requirement
    C. A human resources requirement
    D. A tax requirement

77. When processing personal data, certain things are required. Which of the following is not necessarily required?
    A. A privacy notice
    B. A lawful processing criterion
    C. A response to a data subject's request
    D. Records of processing activities

78. An employee has access to files she was not supposed to access. Which of the following is most likely true?
    A. Since the access was within the organization, it is not a data breach
    B. As soon as the access is discovered, the extent of the access and consequences need to be assessed
    C. Due to the internal leak, the original lawful processing criterion cannot be relied on anymore
    D. Unless the employee shares the data, there is no data breach

79. In case of a data breach, which of the following data processing principles is least likely violated?
    A. Confidentiality
    B. Proportionality
    C. Storage limitation
    D. Purpose limitation

This information can be used for the following four questions:

The data protection authority of one of the member states is conducting an investigation. An organization reported a data breach that potentially resulted in the loss of sensitive personal data of many data subjects.

After the organization suspected that the data was accessible by third parties due to the server configuration, it reported the incident to the data protection authority directly. At this moment the organization is only aware of there having been a possibility for outsiders to access the personal data (some of which was sensitive), and not whether it actually has been accessed or by whom.

The data protection authority found the incident shocking, regardless of whether personal data has been accessed by external parties. Because of that, they started an investigation.

80. The organization reported a data breach without knowing whether an external party accessed personal data. What is legally required of a controller?
    A. A data breach needs to be reported only if sensitive personal data has leaked
    B. Only if adverse consequences for the data subjects manifest themselves does a data breach need to be reported
    C. Only if a data subject complains does the organization need to report the data breach
    D. A data breach needs to be reported without undue delay

81. In this case, what likely has the highest priority of the organization?
    A. The organization should perform background checks on employees
    B. The organization should figure out which personal data has been accessed by external parties
    C. Purchase a new firewall
    D. Purchase a better virus scanner

82. During its investigation, the data protection authority found that the storage on the server was not covered in the organization's data processing inventory. Who is likely held accountable for this?
    A. The organization's CEO
    B. The organization's CIO
    C. The organization's data protection officer
    D. The organization's privacy officer

83. For storing the personal data, what is most likely the lawful processing criterion the organization relies on?
    A. Legitimate interest
    B. The same lawful processing criterion the organization relied on for the collection
    C. Necessary for a contract
    D. Consent

84. An organization finds out it stores personal data since before the GDPR. Which of the following is most likely true?
    A. A new lawful processing criterion is necessary after May 25th 2018
    B. A new lawful processing criterion is necessary after May 25th 2016
    C. The same lawful processing criterion relied on under Directive 95 can be relied on
    D. Whether action needs to be taken depends on whether Binding Corporate Rules are in place

85. A travel agency uses its customers' e-mail addresses for contacting them. Which of the following is the least possible?
    A. The contacting is in line with the collection purpose
    B. The data subject has opted in
    C. The data subject has opted out
    D. The data subject provided consent

86. Which of the following is true regarding consent and the design of the processing of personal data?
    A. The process can continue if consent turns out to practically be irreversible
    B. There needs to be a privacy notice with a point of contact for withdrawing consent
    C. The Privacy by Design principles likely result in the reversibility of consent at the earliest possible moment
    D. Consent for the whole processing is implied if certain parts are optional to achieve the purpose

87. A logistics company's vehicles all send out maintenance indicators and connect with the company and other cars through the internet. This makes scheduling maintenance and planning pickups easier. What is this an example of?
    A. Software as a Service
    B. Biometric processing
    C. The Internet of Things
    D. IP tracking

88. When it concerns the international processing of personal data, when is a controller least likely required to have Binding Corporate Rules or a data processing agreement in place?
    A. A transfer within the organization
    B. A transfer to a non-processor third party
    C. When it concerns data processed by a processor in an adequate country
    D. An organization that does not process sensitive personal data

89. A recruitment agency contacts you regarding a job opening. In which of the following cases is the recruitment agency least likely to rely on the lawful processing criterion legitimate interest?
   A. When using the function of a social media website that allows recruiters to contact people with a certain profile
   B. When browsing social media websites for suitable contacts and contacting them
   C. Going through the database of CVs scraped from job searching websites
   D. When a potential job applicant is in contact with the recruitment agency for another job

90. When an organization uses an employee's personal e-mail address to reach the employee when the employee is on vacation, with a message that is not considered urgent, which of the data processing principles is most likely violated?
   A. Proportionality
   B. Accuracy
   C. Storage limitation
   D. Integrity

Answer key exam 3:

1B, 2A, 3C, 4A, 5A, 6B, 7B, 8A, 9A, 10A, 11A, 12C, 13D, 14A, 15A, 16D, 17B, 18B, 19A, 20A, 21B, 22B, 23B, 24D, 25C, 26D, 27B, 28D, 29D, 30B, 31A, 32C, 33C, 34B, 35D, 36A, 37A, 38A, 39C, 40C, 41A, 42B, 43B, 44C, 45D, 46C, 47D, 48D, 49B, 50B, 51B, 52D, 53A, 54A, 55C, 56B, 57B, 58D, 59D, 60A, 61D, 62A, 63A, 64A, 65D, 66C, 67B, 68D, 69D, 70A, 71A, 72D, 73B, 74A, 75A, 76A, 77A, 78B, 79B, 80D, 81B, 82A, 83B, 84C, 85C, 86C, 87C, 88B, 89A, 90A

Correct answers and explanations for exam 3:

1. EEA stands for European Economic Area. Which of the following best describes the EEA?
   A. A data protection regulation
   B. An international agreement (correct)
   C. A data protection directive
   D. A set of EU member state rules

Info:

B is the correct answer. Although it is not technically an agreement but instead something established through an agreement, 'agreement' fits best of the available options. The European Economic Area is an area consisting of the EU member states, as well as a few others. Free trade is thus extended beyond just the members of the EU.

2. The European single market is sometimes referred to as the common market. Which countries are part of the European single market?
   A. **The EU's member states, Iceland, Liechtenstein, and Norway (correct)**
   B. The EU's member states
   C. The EU's member states and Canada
   D. The EU's member states and the US through Privacy Shield

Info:
A is the correct answer. These are the countries that are part of the European single market. It is important to note that there are more countries in the European single market than just the member states of the EU.

3. European laws go through several institutions. Which institution drafts most laws?
   A. The European parliament
   B. The European council
   C. **The European Commission (correct)**
   D. The member states

Info:
C is the correct answer. The European Commission is the institution that drafts most laws. It does, however, not vote on the laws it drafts.

4. There are many reasons for privacy protection. In a medical context, which of the following is the biggest benefit from increased medical privacy?
   A. **Patients are more open during medical treatment (correct)**
   B. The doctor can process insurance information faster
   C. Fines for violations of privacy
   D. Organizations are less likely to infringe on a person's privacy

Info:

A is the correct answer. When patients know the information they share is protected, they will likely feel more comfortable opening up, and thus the doctor is able to provide better medical care.

5. A construction company puts up a billboard on its construction site, proudly announcing which celebrity will own the building. Which of the following is true?
   A. **The construction company needs a valid lawful processing criterion to advertise this way (correct)**
   B. Celebrity names are in the public domain, and therefore are not personal data
   C. Consent for this advertisement is implied in signing the construction contract
   D. If the advertising was based on consent, it need not be reversible, because of the significant cost of the billboard

Info:

A is the correct answer. For any sharing of personal data, whether already public or not, a controller needs a lawful processing criterion to be met. The fact that the celebrities are going to live in that building says something about those celebrities and is personal data, and the construction company can't just use it any way it pleases.

6. Which court, also known as the Strasbourg court, judges cases beyond the EU regarding the European Convention of Human rights?
   A. The European Court of Justice
   B. The European Court of Human Rights (correct)
   C. The European Peace Court
   D. The Member states' national court

Info:
B is the correct answer. Keep in mind, the Council of Europe and the European Court of Human Rights are not institutions of the EU.

7. In 2006 the Data Retention Directive was passed. Under the Data Retention Directive, which of the following is correct?
   A. An e-mail must be stored for at least 24 months
   B. An IP address must be stored for at least six months (correct)
   C. Telecommunication is exempt from retention
   D. It was amended by the Directive on Privacy and Electronic Communications

Info:
B is the correct answer. This is actually a measure that does not protect privacy. You might be annoyed by the level of detail of this question. There will be several questions like this, but don't let not knowing these details discourage you (you are allowed to miss a few answers).

8. Spam is a nuisance for many. Regarding the regulation of spam in the EU, where would you look?
   A. The e-privacy directive (correct)
   B. CAN-SPAM
   C. The Data Protection Directive
   D. The Data Retention Directive

Info:
A is the correct answer. The e-privacy directive concerns telecommunication, which includes spam (the electronic part at least). CAN-SPAM also pertains to spam, but not in the EU.

9. You visit an anonymous support group. Attendants are asked to create a nickname. Which of the following is most likely true?

   A. If the nickname is linked to a phone number or e-mail address, it is personal data (correct)

   B. A nickname by itself can never constitute personal data

   C. A nickname by itself always constitutes personal data

   D. Use of the nickname requires consent

Info:

A is the correct answer. The phone number and e-mail address themselves are quite revealing, and linked with the e-mail or phone number the nickname can likely be traced back to a single person (making that person identifiable).

10. A data subject is the subject of personal data. Which of the following is least likely considered a data subject?

   A. The person that was the source for anonymous data (correct)

   B. An element of a data set

   C. The person part of a contract, not the one the lawful processing criterion "necessary for the performance of a contract"

   D. A person listed on a website

Info:

A is the correct answer. When the data is anonymous, it cannot be traced back to anyone. Regardless of whether someone supplied it, if it cannot be traced back to someone, there is no data subject. Option B is vague and debatable, but option A is clear and therefore more correct than B.

11. A controller determines the means and purposes of the processing. Which of the following is the best description of this?
    A. **The final responsible for what happens to personal data processing-wise (correct)**
    B. The designer of the security measures
    C. A party of the data processing agreement
    D. A party requesting another party to process personal data

Info:
A is the correct answer. The controller determines the means and purposes, so unless there is a disobedient processor for which it can reasonably be expected that the controller cannot be blamed, the controller remains ultimately responsible for what happens. The other three descriptions are less complete because they focus only on one specific aspect.

12. The European Data Protection Board issues guidance from time to time. Which of the following is now required when using standard contractual clauses?
    A. A data protection impact assessment
    B. A data processing agreement
    C. **A transfer impact assessment (correct)**
    D. A privacy assessment

Info:
C is the correct answer. A transfer impact assessment can be seen as a data protection impact assessment specific to the transfer of personal data to a third country. So, if a controller transfers personal data to a country outside of the EU, a transfer impact assessment needs to be performed periodically, where for example the level of protection provided by the laws in the third country is assessed in the context of the processing that takes place.

13. In a large organization, which department is most likely to order a privacy program?
    A. The privacy department
    B. The IT department
    C. The marketing department
    D. The compliance department (correct)

Info:

D is the correct answer. The compliance department likely occupies itself with compliance with applicable laws and regulations. A privacy program would fit that purpose. The other options are also possible if the organization does not have a compliance department.

14. Which of the following is the least true regarding the right to object?
    A. After receipt of the request, the controller must act immediately (correct)
    B. The request to block processing for direct marketing is absolute
    C. Data subjects can object to processing for scientific research
    D. Data subjects can object to processing for the controller's legitimate interest

Info:

A is the correct answer. The controller has one month to act. This means one month to provide all the information. If there is a good reason to extend this one month there are exceptions. The other options also are correct in many cases, but option A is correct in all cases.

15. There are four defined classes of privacy. Which of the following is not one of them?
    A. Medical privacy (correct)
    B. Bodily privacy
    C. Territorial privacy
    D. Information privacy

Info:

A is the correct answer. Medical privacy sounds like a class of privacy, and perhaps can be seen as one, but it is not the answer here. You can see that medical privacy is more specific than the other three options, and is a sub-class of bodily privacy (or even information privacy). Admittedly, this question is misleading/flawed, as will some of the questions on the real exam be.

16. The Justices of the Peace Act enacted in 1361 contained a certain level of privacy protection. How was this included?
    A. The army was forbidden to enter civilian houses
    B. Tax collectors were limited by law
    C. Churches were forbidden to keep records
    D. The arrest of peeping Toms (correct)

Info:

D is the correct answer. The Justices of Peace Act includes protection against peeping Toms. It also includes protection against eavesdroppers.

17. Which country implemented the first data protection law that took the potential of IT developments into account?
    A. Belgium
    B. Germany (correct)
    C. Austria
    D. The United States

Info:

B is the correct answer. This would be in Germany, and more specifically in Hesse. Don't stress if you don't know the details to this extent. Although there will be questions that require this level of detail, there is a chance you have remembered the relevant details, guessed correctly, or have a score high enough to miss a question or two.

18. There are many public sources for personal data. Which of the following is true for public personal data?
    A. Public personal data can be processed without restrictions
    B. Public personal data can be processed based on consent (correct)
    C. A controller never needs to provide a privacy notice for public personal data
    D. Processing of public personal data does not have to be recorded in the data processing inventory

Info:

B is the correct answer. It might seem illogical since it is public, but for public personal data you still need an applicable lawful processing criterion (and, unless there is a good reason not to, provide a privacy notice). One of the lawful processing criteria is consent, so if you have obtained consent you can rely on this lawful processing criterion. Of course, it is unrealistic to look for the data subjects of public personal data and ask for consent, but it is possible and therefore the correct answer (as the others are not correct).

19. A retailer has a wealth of data of its customers, all collected to complete the sales. What is true regarding further use of this data?
   A. **The retailer can further process the data when only the elements are used that result in a sufficiently high level of data aggregation (correct)**
   B. The retailer is free to sell the full data for research, as that is a legitimate interest
   C. The retailer would require consent to use anonymized data further, which would then lead to satisfying the lawful processing criterion
   D. The retailer would require a legal obligation to further process anonymous data

Info:
A is the correct answer. A sufficiently high level of data aggregation implies that it is no longer personal data. Although it is not explicit, it would not be sufficiently high if the customers were identifiable, hence the term sufficiently high implies certain conditions are satisfied. Although option A is perhaps vague and complicated to comprehend in the context, the other options are clearly incorrect.

20. A company has a privacy policy on its website, for both guiding employees and informing data subjects. Which of the following is true?
   A. **The privacy policy is likely too complicated to count as a privacy notice (correct)**
   B. The employees don't require further information
   C. A privacy notice needs to be provided prior to processing
   D. The policy is likely suitable to convey the organization's attitude to personal data processing

Info:
A is the correct answer. If the privacy policy is also used to guide employees (note that guiding is different from informing), it likely contains too much information to be readable enough for the data subjects. See Article 12 (1) of the GDPR, which requires conciseness.

21. A store collects phone IDs through Bluetooth scanning and tracks its customers as they move through the store. Which of the following is a danger?
   A. The employees that are aware of the practice won't be able to avoid being monitored
   B. The store can link the customer's purchases to the phone ID (correct)
   C. There is no way to capture the practice into a privacy notice
   D. Consent is required from the employees in order to use the practice

Info:

B is the correct answer. If the store links the purchase times recorded in the cash register to the phone ID that was at the cash register at that time, it is clear which purchase belongs to which phone ID. If payment is done electronically, this also links the phone ID to other information.

22. A shopping mall offers free WIFI. However, users need to consent to being tracked and provide their full names. Which of the following is most likely true?
    A. The controller requires the full name, otherwise, it cannot reverse the consent
    B. **The consent is not valid, and the WIFI needs to be provided without consent or not at all (correct)**
    C. The consent can be valid but depends on the retention period
    D. The shopping mall is free to collect the data it wants even without consent

Info:

B is the correct answer. There are many issues here, but one of them is that consent is a condition for free WIFI, which might not be freely given. Another issue is that not every data subject is likely to see the consequences of being tracked, and therefore the consent is possibly not clear enough. Option D could also be correct since it mentions data instead of personal data, but from the consent mentioned in the question, it is already clear that personal data is involved, meaning the shopping mall is restricted in its collection.

23. A dating app sells the personal data it gathers. What is true about the privacy notice?
   A. This practice can reasonably be expected and needs no explicit mentioning
   B. It needs to clearly mention that your personal data is being sold, which personal data, and to whom (correct)
   C. Selling the personal data is required for the lawful processing criterion necessary for a contract
   D. A privacy notice is not necessary if the controller is based in the US

Info:

B is the correct answer. Article 13 of the GDPR specifies that information on (categories of) recipients need to be provided, and Article 12 specifies this information needs to be transparent and intelligible. These combine into the requirement to clearly specify that your personal data is being sold and what is done with it, as well as the (categories) of third parties your personal data is being sold to.

24. An international organization can opt to use Binding Corporate Rules for international transfers of personal data. Of the following, which least suffices as Binding Corporate Rules?
   A. A copy of the GDPR
   B. The internal security standards
   C. A privacy notice
   D. A Bring Your Own Device policy (correct)

Info:

D is the correct answer. A bring your own device policy does least likely specify the rules of international processing of personal data within the organization. The GDPR, for example, is technically correct (although practically unlikely), the internal security standards will also apply to personal data and therefore could contain all requirements, and the privacy notice theoretically could contain all relevant information. This question is horrible, but you need to be ready for one or two strange questions like this.

This information can be used for the following five questions:

A service company maintains and operates a large campus where multiple companies are operating. It concerns a collection of factories and offices, fully surrounded by a fence. The property is owned by the service company.

The service company maintains all roads and buildings. Only the maintenance of one of the renter's plants is done by the company that built and operates the plant. The IT infrastructure is also maintained by the service company.

All users of the campus, at the individual employee level, are known to the service company. This is because of safety procedures, which legally require the service company to know who is present on-site. Everybody entering the site has a personal ID badge or a visitor badge linked to a copy of an identity card.

To improve safety, and address concerns regarding reckless behavior, the service company monitors all persons on the campus. This is done through CCTV, but the security staff also uses speeding cameras and issues a warning to the person linked to the license plate of the speeding vehicle.

25. In order to use CCTV, which of the following least likely needed to be done first?
    A. A data protection impact assessment
    B. Update the data processing inventory
    C. Adjust the privacy notice on the website (correct)
    D. Determine the appropriate retention period

Info:

C is the correct answer. When entering a property where CCTV is used, it does not warn you enough when only the website contains the privacy notice. There will need to be a sign before entering the CCTV-monitored area. A privacy notice can (and sometimes needs to) be in a different form than information on a website. The user needs to be able to be informed, and the form of this information will need to be accessible to the user. Someone delivering a package to the campus, for example, is not going to visit the website to read the privacy notice, and will need to be informed through a sign when entering the premises.

26. In order to send a warning to the person linked to the license plate after a violation, which of the following lawful processing criteria is most likely applicable?
    A. Consent
    B. Vital interest
    C. Contract
    D. Legitimate interest (correct)

Info:

D is the correct answer. If a balancing between the organization's interest (safety of its employees, for example) and the privacy of the data subject, then legitimate interest could apply. Consent would not be freely given (not freely given, because it would be required for work), and vital interests are not directly in danger. A contract could perhaps apply, but the controller here is the service company, not the employer, and if since the feature is new it is clear that it is not "necessary" for the performance of a contract (although it is the second-best option).

27. When linking a visitor badge to an individual, which of the following is most likely true?
    A. All relevant details can only be processed when consent is provided
    B. **Making a copy of a person's ID card is unnecessary (correct)**
    C. The person's national tax ID is sufficient
    D. A full copy of the ID card can be processed

Info:

B is the correct option. Making a copy of an ID card is invasive. Unless legally required, seeing the ID card to verify someone's identity is sufficient.

28. Regarding the storage period of the information collected on the visitors, which of the following is most likely true?
    A. Storage can be based on backup retention periods
    B. Storage should be indefinite, as something can always be needed
    C. The retention period can be extended if another useful way of processing personal data comes up
    D. **The storage period is linked to the lawful processing criterion (correct)**

Info:

D is the correct answer. In order to process the personal data (the information of the visitor), there needs to be a lawful processing criterion that is applicable. That lawful processing criterion is linked to a purpose. When that purpose has been fulfilled (for example, when the legal retention period has passed, or when the visitor has left), the lawful processing criterion no longer applies and the personal data can no longer be processed. This means the personal data will need to be deleted (keeping it means storing it, and storing is also processing).

29. Which of the following of the service company's practices is not multi-factor authentication?
    A. Scanning a badge and showing an ID
    B. An account working only on a certain computer
    C. Scanning the badge and typing a passcode
    D. Checking if the shown ID belongs to the person showing it (correct)

Info:

D is the correct answer. An ID is (likely) only one identifier, thus this is single-factor authentication. The other options look at multiple factors.

30. An organization can improve data protection by implementing safeguards. Which is not a main type of safeguard?
    A. Administrative safeguard
    B. Detective safeguard (correct)
    C. Technical safeguard
    D. Physical safeguard

Info:

B is the correct answer. There are detective controls, but not detective safeguards.

31. Which of the following are the information life cycle principles?
    A. Collection, Use, Disclosure, Storage, and Destruction (correct)
    B. Processing, Use, Disclosure, Storage, and Destruction
    C. Collection, Processing, Disclosure, Storage, and Destruction
    D. Collection, Processing, Retention, and Disclosure

Info:

A is the correct answer. These are the four principles of the information life cycle. The other options are similar, but have one or more elements changed incorrectly.

32. There are several models of privacy protection. Which of the following is not a model of privacy protection?
    A. Comprehensive model
    B. Sectoral model
    C. Technical determinist model (correct)
    D. Co-regulatory model

Info:

C is the correct answer. Comprehensive (covering all aspects), sectoral (arranged per sector) and co-regulatory (composed in cooperation with industry) are the models of privacy you need to know. Technical determinist is not something you need to be aware of, and it is a made-up term. Self-regulation is not part of the options, but this is where industries regulate themselves by composing their own guidelines/rules.

33. Which of the following is least true regarding Binding Corporate Rules?
    A. The organization needs to be based in the EU
    B. They are legally binding
    C. It replaces data processing agreements (correct)
    D. The data protection authority can judge the Binding Corporate Rules to be inadequate

Info:

C is the correct answer. Binding corporate rules are meant for within an international organization, and thus do not replace contracts regarding processing by processors (third parties processing on behalf of the organization).

34. Which of the following is not a description of a risk?
   A. Threat x Vulnerability x Expected loss
   B. A negative occurrence (correct)
   C. The chance of a data breach
   D. The chance of a lost USB stick being accessed

Info:

B is the correct answer. Risk is the likelihood multiplied by a negative occurrence, meaning how high the chance is that the negative consequence really happens. A negative occurrence is something that has already happened, so this is not a risk but a risk that has already manifested itself. The other options describe something that has not happened yet.

35. Of the following, which is not a basic principle of role-based access control?
   A. Segregation of duties
   B. Least privilege
   C. Need to know or access
   D. Hierarchy approval (correct)

Info:

D is the correct answer. Hierarchy approval (approval needed by, for example, management) is not a principle of role-based access control. Role-based access control describes who has access to certain information, but not necessarily who needs to approve the access.

36. There are several ways of identifying someone through technology. How is it called when the settings of someone's browser are used to identify someone?
    A. **Browser fingerprinting (correct)**
    B. Technical identification
    C. A browser leak
    D. Phishing

Info:

A is the correct answer. Browser settings consist of many elements, and are quite different, resulting in each browser having a (close to) unique combination of settings. This uniqueness leads to the comparison with a fingerprint, which can be used to identify the browser that opens a website.

37. The GDPR requires protection for certain types of data. Which of the following least likely requires protection?
    A. **An organization's list of business-to-business contracts consisting of functional mailboxes (correct)**
    B. An American tourist's personal data
    C. A mildly aggregated database with personal data
    D. A pseudonymized list of test subject data

Info:

A is the correct answer. A functional mailbox is a mailbox that is not linked to a person. Therefore, unless the organization only has one employee, for example, the address of the functional mailbox does not constitute personal data and does not require protection under the GDPR.

38. Which of the following is least likely true regarding the relationship between a processor and a data subject?
   A. **A processor is responsible for complying with a data access request (correct)**
   B. The processor has a responsibility towards the data subject regarding secure processing of personal data
   C. The processor has no responsibility towards the data subject regarding the data processing agreement
   D. A data subject can ask a processor to provide the name of the controller

Info:
A is the correct answer. The processor is not responsible for complying with the data access request, but the controller is responsible. Of course, the controller can instruct the processor to fulfill the request, but the controller remains responsible.

39. Which of the following is least likely true regarding sensitive personal data?
   A. A higher level of protection is required compared to that for non-sensitive personal data
   B. A different lawful processing criterion is needed than for personal data processed relying on legitimate interest
   C. **Consent is the only possible lawful processing criterion (correct)**
   D. There is a difference between the restrictions on newly generated sensitive personal data and public sensitive personal data

Info:
C is the correct answer. Although consent is generally required, Article 9 of the GDPR describes exceptions, such as for reasons of substantial public interest or scientific research.

40. Which of the following requires the processing of personal data?
   A. Processing a list of highly aggregated data
   B. Publishing all third parties in the privacy notice
   C. Providing a privacy notice to a mailing list (correct)
   D. Formatting a cloud space

Info:

C is the correct answer. In order to supply the mailing list with the privacy notice, the mailing list itself has to be used. The use of the mailing list can be considered processing of personal data (the personal data being the e-mail addresses). For this reason, it is desirable to provide the privacy notice before someone signs up for a mailing list.

41. Of the following, which is least likely required for the completion of a contract to which the data subject is a party?
   A. A list of public data being processed at the request of a third-party (correct)
   B. The fulfillment of a retail order
   C. Being part of an employer's database
   D. Food delivery

Info:

A is the correct answer. The data subjects on the list of public data are likely not part of the contract. Since this lawful processing criterion requires the data subject to be part of the contract, this lawful processing criterion cannot be relied on for the processing of the list of public data. Admittedly, it can be difficult to see what exactly is asked due to the phrasing of the question, which is something you'll encounter on the exam as well.

42. The field of artificial intelligence has been making significant progress. Which of the following is least likely a privacy risk linked to artificial intelligence?
   A. New personal data is generated easily, by combining and analyzing data
   B. Consent is obtained in unclear ways, leading to overprocessing of personal data (correct)
   C. Personal data gets processed outside of the originally understood scope
   D. Encryption can prove less reliable as a security measure

Info:

B is the correct answer. Before allowing artificial intelligence to process personal data, consent should be obtained. This consent should meet all the requirements. Therefore, if it was possible to obtain consent at all, it has not been obtained in an unclear way. The answer here is quite theoretical, and you'll have to understand that what exactly the answer claims (and the implications things like having obtained consent have). Notice the similarity of this question to a question on one of the other exams in this document, and how the answers are only slightly different and don't be tricked into automatically choosing the same answer for both questions.

This information can be used for the following four questions:

Recently you have been appointed the role of privacy officer at an international social media company. You work in a team with three other privacy officers, and you report to the CEO.

The social media company is not from the EU but has a website in almost every EU country, including the ability to translate text to the local language. No payments are required from users, but corporate pages cost money and can only be paid in US dollars.

Given how new the regulation is, you and your colleagues disagree on the interpretation from time to time. Whenever a disagreement arises, the CEO eventually chooses the most desirable interpretation.

Although you notice that your colleagues' translation from law to practice often stems from your poor understanding of technology, the CIO often sides with them.

43. After another disagreement with your colleagues, your boss accuses you of not doing what is best for the company. Which of the following is true regarding disciplining a privacy officer?
    A. The GDPR provides protection against privacy officers being disciplined due to doing their job
    B. **The company can discipline the privacy officer, as long as no labor laws are broken (correct)**
    C. Only if the performance is bad, does the GDPR not restrict a change in role as a form of discipline
    D. An appraisal containing criticism on the privacy officer's social skills are intolerable in this context

Info:
B is the correct answer. A privacy officer is not a data protection officer and is not protected as described in Article 38 (3) of the GDPR. Therefore, as long as no other laws (such as labor laws) are broken, disciplining is acceptable (for example for poor performance or violations).

44. From a privacy perspective, what can likely not be said about you reporting to the CIO?
    A. The CEO will be fully responsible for privacy
    B. The privacy officers will not be held responsible for decisions taken by management
    C. **The CIO will be fully competent to make decisions regarding the allocation of budget (correct)**
    D. The GDPR does not allow for the CIO to balance limited means between privacy and security

Info:

C is the correct answer. The CIO has corporate interests which he/she has to balance with privacy interests. This can result in privacy not receiving the attention it requires to comply with the GDPR. For this reason, a data protection officer would report to the CEO (who is generally above the CIO).

45. The social media company uses web beacons on other websites to see which of its users visit these websites. Which of the following is least likely true?
    A. This practice can be considered monitoring
    B. A data protection impact assessment is needed before starting the use of the web beacon
    C. There needs to be a proper balance between the invasiveness of the practice and the benefits it provides to the social media company and the users
    D. **Data subjects do not need to be informed by the websites containing the web beacons (correct)**

Info:

D is the correct answer. If the website that the user visits has a web beacon loaded from a third party (the social media company), then this constitutes transferring personal data to third parties. This is something the visitor needs to be made aware of before it happens (so the web beacon cannot be loaded before the privacy notice has been read and a lawful processing criterion is applicable).

46. Given that the web beacon is also placed on sites of a political or sexual nature, what is likely the only lawful processing criterion that can be relied on?
    A. Legitimate interest
    B. Contract
    C. **Consent (correct)**
    D. Vital interest

Info:
C is the correct answer. Linking a visit to a website of a sexual or political nature possibly exposes a sexual or political preference, and can therefore be seen as sensitive personal data. For this reason, consent is likely required (see Article 9 of the GDPR).

47. An organization processes personal data, and during that processing, the legally required retention period gets longer. Which of the following is least likely true?
    A. The storage limitation is respected, despite the change in the retention period
    B. Given the extended retention period, the accuracy of the personal data is likelier to be negatively affected
    C. The data processing inventory will need to be updated
    D. **Despite the longer retention period, the given consent remains valid (correct)**

Info:
D is the correct answer. Consent needs to be specific, which likely means that the initial consent was specific about the retention period. Therefore, if the retention period specified during the initial consent extends beyond what the controller expected and communicated, the initial consent is no longer valid. This is a bit of a tricky situation though, since the legally required retention period implies a lawful processing criterion different from consent, hence consent might not even be required. Option B makes sense if you consider that the more time passes, for example, a data subject's address can change, affecting the accuracy of the personal data.

48. Which of the following is most likely true about the processing of sensitive personal data?
    A. Only information provided by the data subject can be considered sensitive personal data
    B. Consent is the only way to process sensitive personal data
    C. Only explicit information can reveal sensitive personal data
    D. Even if false, something can still be considered sensitive personal data (correct)

Info:

D is the correct answer. Just because a piece of information about someone is false, doesn't mean it is not considered personal data. The same goes for sensitive personal data. For example, if a social media website guesses someone's sexual preference based on that user's behavior, this is sensitive personal data even if the sexual preference is guessed incorrectly.

49. The EU institutions have their own regulation. On which lawful processing criterion can the EU institutions not rely?
    A. Consent
    B. Legitimate interest (correct)
    C. Legal obligation
    D. Public interest

Info:

B is the correct answer. Regulation 2018/1725 is the law applicable to the EU institutions, and Article 5 specifies the lawful processing criteria. However, legitimate interest is not a lawful processing criterion available to the EU institutions. There will be a question or two like this on your exam, where it is unreasonable to expect that you know the answer.

50. When placing cookies, which of the following is most true?
   A. A privacy notice must be provided before placing any cookies
   B. **If the user does not agree to the cookies, processing of personal data through cookies cannot take place and some services may not function (correct)**
   C. For placing a third-party web beacon, the user can simply be referred to the third party after placing the web beacon
   D. No cookies are allowed without a lawful processing criterion

Info:
B is the correct answer. A visitor (data subject) can object to the processing of his/her personal data, and if the objection is justified the processing must stop. This goes for personal data processed by placing cookies as well. Note that not all cookies result in the processing of personal data, so it will only apply to the cookies that lead to the processing of personal data.

51. Which of the following is not a risk of not properly identifying a data subject for an access request?
   A. Unlawful processing
   B. **Losing the original lawful processing criterion/criteria (correct)**
   C. Someone other than the data subject sees the personal data
   D. A data breach

Info:
B is the correct answer. When you lose the original lawful processing criterion/criteria you are no longer allowed to process (or even keep) the personal data. This has nothing to do with a data access request or the identification during that access request.

52. You rent a car and afterward find out that the rental agency placed you on a mailing list. What likely happened if this comes as a surprise?
    A. You were not shown a layered privacy notice
    B. No consent was obtained
    C. A data access request was not complied with
    D. **You were not provided with the opportunity to opt-out (correct)**

Info:

D is the correct answer. When you are provided with the opportunity to opt out, this should be clear. In this case, you are not aware of being placed on the mailing list, therefore there was likely no opportunity to opt-out (or you would have seen it, making you aware).

53. Cloud services are becoming more and more popular. Which of the following is an example of cloud computing?
    A. **A web-based e-mail service (correct)**
    B. Use of a modem
    C. Having mainframes connected
    D. Using a virtual private network

Info:

A is the correct answer. If the e-mail service is web-based, means the computing takes place on a different computer and the data is on a server. A simple definition of cloud computing is computing services provided over the internet, either storage or the running of applications (try to see the practical meaning of this definition to help you pick the correct answer). Option A fits that definition.

54. After renting a car, the rental agency sends you a fine because the car's GPS signaled that you crossed a national border (which costs extra). What could you have expected before?
   A. Information about GPS information being processed (correct)
   B. Information about paying fines
   C. The possibility to opt-out of receiving a fine
   D. A detailed list of third parties involved

Info:

A is the correct answer. The rental agency links your GPS to the car, which is linked to you for the period you rented it. This is therefore the processing of personal data, and you would have needed to be informed before the rental agency performed this processing (most likely when you signed the rental agreement).

55. An international organization in both the middle east and the EU has a set of internal guidelines on how to deal with processing personal data in a manner compliant with all applicable laws. What would this set of guidelines likely be called?
   A. A privacy notice
   B. A privacy policy
   C. Binding Corporate Rules (correct)
   D. Privacy Shield

Info:

C is the correct answer. This is a clear example of binding corporate rules. If Privacy Shield was still allowed to be used and the organization was in the US instead of the middle east, then perhaps this could have been a correct answer as well. A privacy policy might seem like a correct answer as well, but policies are too general to cover all the requirements in sufficient detail.

56. Works councils can have an impact on the level of privacy in an organization. Of the following, where would a works council most likely have input?
    A. Updating the organization's privacy notice
    B. Installing CCTV cameras necessary for security (correct)
    C. Updating the organization's privacy policy
    D. Processing employee data using new payroll software

Info:

B is the correct answer. Installing CCTV cameras can be quite invasive. Since the input of the work councils is often required for significant changes in labor conditions, the invasive practice of installing CCTV cameras likely requires the input of the work council.

57. Of the following, what is the least likely lawful processing criterion to rely on as an employer processing personal data of employees?
    A. Legitimate interest
    B. Consent (correct)
    C. Contract
    D. Legal obligation

Info:

B is the correct answer. Relying on consent is not a good idea for an employer. The employer/employee relationship can prove problematic for giving consent freely. Employers will possibly experience pressure to consent, regardless of whether that pressure is real or not.

58. Some devices can be unlocked using a fingerprint. Which of the following complies most with the Privacy by Design principles?
    A. Making a connection with a secure server to verify the print
    B. Encrypting the print
    C. Using salting
    D. **Storing the print on the device (correct)**

Info:

D is the correct answer. When the fingerprint is stored on the device, no external connections need to be made, meaning less risk of interception. In addition, when the fingerprints of all devices are stored on a server, for example, the entire collection of fingerprints might be leaked if the security is breached. Therefore, in this situation, and with the information provided, D is the correct answer.

59. Bring Your Own Device practices are becoming more and more popular. Which of the following best describes Bring Your Own Device?
    A. A situation where employees bring their own work laptop home to connect over a VPN
    B. Software to check corporate e-mail through a web browser
    C. CIO approval of the privacy policy
    D. **Employees voluntarily using a private device to perform work tasks (correct)**

Info:

D is the correct answer. The key to 'bring your own device' is that the employees use private devices (regardless of whether they bring them or buy them). The voluntary element in option D is not necessary and is placed there to mislead, but it still fits the best description of the options available.

60. There are several risks to take into account when implementing a whistleblowing program. Which of the following is the least likely risk?

A. A wrongly addressed e-mail to the whistleblower (correct)

B. Endangering the whistleblower by requiring disclosed of his/her identity

C. Risking false data on a data subject when allowing anonymous whistleblowing

D. Endangering those involved by not restricting access to the data sufficiently

Info:

A is the correct answer. The whistleblower is the one whose identity needs to be hidden, hence accidentally sending him/her an e-mail is not the most likely risk (although that depends on the content of the e-mail, because if it provides new information on the accused this is also bad).

61. Some companies perform a constant real-time check on what happens with the personal data they process. What can this be called?

A. Surveillance

B. Constant processing

C. Data retention

D. Monitoring (correct)

Info:

D is the correct answer. Monitoring is the correct term here. A simplified definition of monitoring can be constantly evaluating/assessing something.

62. When processors and processors of processors (sub-processors) are involved, which of the following is most likely true?
    A. **All processing parties that are not the controller will need to sign a data processing agreement (correct)**
    B. When Binding Corporate Rules are in place, there is no need to sign a data processing agreement
    C. The controller is only responsible for the consequences of the actions of direct processors
    D. What needs to be signed depends on the country in which the processing takes place

Info:
A is the correct answer. Sub-processors also need to be part of the data processing agreement. The controller is responsible and needs to ensure that all parties process in a way compliant with the applicable privacy requirements, including processors that are hired by its processors.

63. When a government agency installs CCTV to monitor suspicious activity, which lawful processing criterion is least likely applicable?
    A. **Consent (correct)**
    B. Public task
    C. Legitimate interest
    D. Legal requirement

Info:
A is the correct answer. Consent to monitoring suspicious activity kind of defeats the purpose because those being monitored will be aware and the suspicious activity is less likely to be adequately monitored.

64. The GDPR introduced fines of as high as EUR 20 million or 4% of annual worldwide turnover. Which of the following is least likely going to result in a fine?
   A. **A wrongfully addressed e-mail (correct)**
   B. A systematic security flaw
   C. A wrongful processing
   D. A data breach due to negligence of management

Info:

A is the correct answer. A wrongfully addressed e-mail is least preventable of the options provided, and therefore least likely to result in a fine (although, depending on the content of the e-mail, barriers to human error can be expected to be implemented).

65. An organization can audit its privacy practices. How can a privacy audit best be described?
   A. A check on the availability of data protection impact assessments where needed
   B. A thorough inspection of the data processing inventory
   C. A team appointed by the CIO verifying the security standards
   D. **An independent assessment of the compliance with the relevant framework (correct)**

Info:

D is the correct answer. An audit is an examination/assessment (in this case of the compliance with the privacy rules), and a privacy audit only makes sense if it is done independently. Therefore, D answers the question best.

66. When a processor collects personal data on behalf of a controller, which of the following is least likely true?
    A. The data subject needs to be shown a privacy notice
    B. The processor collects personal data beyond what is necessary for the purpose of the controller
    C. **If the processor collects additional personal data for its own purposes, the controller is responsible (correct)**
    D. The controller determines how the processor collects personal data, and thus needs a lawful processing criterion to be applicable

Info:

C is the correct answer. When the processor collects personal data for its own purposes, that processor becomes a controller for the personal data it collected for its own purposes. This also means that a lawful processing criterion needs to be applicable because the processor cannot rely on the lawful processing criterion the controller relies on for the personal data it instructed the processor to collect.

This information can be used for the following four questions:

A zoo has recently opened up a children's section where it allows kids to pet all the animals. Kids can be dropped off, and the parents can have some time for themselves. Every kid entering will receive a bracelet with a GPS to monitor where they are, so they will never get lost, and the parents can find their kids quickly.

As soon as a child enters the children's section, an actor in a crocodile suit will stand next to the child and a photo will be taken. The photo can later be purchased as a souvenir. Some children are shy, so the actor in the crocodile suit grabs their hands and positions them in front of the camera.

In addition to several supervisors, there are CCTV cameras throughout the zoo. The recordings are accessible for all staff employees, which is necessary because recordings are studied to figure out animal behavior.

67. Regarding the photograph taken of the child, which of the following is least likely true?
    A. A data access request should provide a copy of the photo taken
    B. **The positioning of the children fits the legitimate interest in the zoo (correct)**
    C. Consent from the parents would have to be obtained before taking the photo
    D. The zoo will need to choose a proportionate retention period for the photo taken

Info:

B is the correct answer. Given the actor having to somewhat pressure the children to be in the photograph can be seen as an objection, and therefore the interest of the child (data subject) outweighs that of the zoo, and the legitimate interest criterion is not applicable.

68. The data protection officer has some doubts regarding the level of access to the CCTV recordings. Which of the following is least likely true regarding this situation?
    A. The CEO will be responsible for taking the correct action
    B. If the data protection officer provides information to the CEO, there is no legal obligation to stop
    C. The organization does not have to provide the data protection officer permanent access to the CCTV recordings
    D. If found to be disproportionate, the data protection officer can restrict access to the CCTV recordings (correct)

Info:
D is the correct answer. Option D does seem to make sense, but unfortunately, the data protection officer has no power to restrict access. The only thing the data protection officer can do is advise, and that is why the data protection officer should have access to the highest level of management. The highest level of management is ultimately responsible, and therefore should be informed of (serious) violations where management needs to intervene.

69. The zoo has a privacy notice on its website, and the specifics are mentioned under all different activities. What can this likely be called?
    A. Privacy by Design
    B. Privacy by Default
    C. A just-in-time notice
    D. A layered privacy notice (correct)

Info:
D is the correct answer. Mentioning the specifics (the relevant information) only under the relevant activities means that the information is only provided when searching for that activity (usually by selecting it through clicking on it). These different sets of information per activity can be seen as layers. Therefore, this is a layered privacy notice.

70. The zoo owns an aquarium as well, located abroad, and named differently. In addition, the zoo uses a third party to manage the aquarium. Which of the following is most likely true if personal data is processed?

A. For the zoo's aquarium, Binding Corporate Rules are sufficient, but with the third party a data processing agreement has to be signed (correct)

B. Binding Corporate Rules are sufficient for any processing of personal data

C. A data protection impact assessment is sufficient for any processing of personal data

D. Nothing is required if the third party managing the aquarium is in a country that is deemed adequate

Info:

A is the correct answer. The managing third party is external, and therefore likely needs to be considered a processor. Processors need to sign a data processing agreement if they process personal data on behalf of the controller.

71. Passwords for websites are generally stored by making them unreadable for those who can assess them. What is this called?

A. Hashing (correct)

B. Salting

C. A firewall

D. Role-based access control

Info:

A is the correct answer. Hashing is the replacing of the characters in a password with different characters. It can also involve changing the number of characters. This way, the hash of the password (so the code after hashing) cannot be changed back into the password (unless it is guessed correctly, which is possible for simple passwords).

72. There are many ways in which an organization can be hijacked by hackers. Which of the following is the least direct cause of this?
    A. Installed malware
    B. A social engineering attack
    C. A database of stolen passwords
    D. An outdated virus scanner (correct)

Info:

D is the correct answer. Here the question is not how likely the options are to be successful, but how directly they can lead to a hijack. An outdated virus scanner can be a broken barrier, but it is not a direct cause because there will still need to be a hijack attempt. Option C might also not seem direct, but it is more direct than option D since the database of passwords is likely stolen with malicious intentions.

73. Geolocation allows a controller to see where a data subject is or has been. Which of the following is least likely used to determine someone's location?
    A. IP address
    B. A web beacon (correct)
    C. GPS
    D. Multi-factor authentication

Info:

B is the correct answer. A web beacon would reveal an IP address but is only useful when loaded. In addition, if the web beacon is loaded the rest of the website is also loaded, so only using the web beacon makes no sense. This question is admittedly multi-interpretable, and several answers can be correct depending on the reasoning you use. You will encounter this on the exam as well, and you will have to follow the most likely train of thought (which here is that the web beacon is more indirect than the other options, and the assumption is that one of the factors of the multi-factor authentication is the location).

74. Not all countries have received an adequacy decision. Who/what/which of the following issues adequacy decisions?
    A. The European Commission (correct)
    B. The European Parliament
    C. The European Data Protection Authority
    D. The Member State authorities

Info:

A is the correct answer. The European Commission is the institution that issues (adopts) adequacy decisions. It does involve an opinion of the European Data Protection Board and the approval of the representatives of the member states, but the European Commission adopts the adequacy decision.

75. Many people are bothered by the marketing practices of organizations. Which law would likely provide the biggest hindrance for controllers to send marketing to home addresses in the EU?
    A. The GDPR (correct)
    B. The e-privacy directive
    C. CAN-SPAM
    D. Directive 95

Info:

A is the correct answer. If it concerns home addresses it concerns physical mail. This does not fall under the e-privacy directive, since it is not electronic. CAN-SPAM is a law in the US, and Directive 95 has been replaced by the GDPR. Therefore, the GDPR remains the only likely option.

76. A controller can have a legal obligation to process certain personal data. Which of the following is the least likely source of such legal obligation?
   A. **A customer requirement (correct)**
   B. A financial requirement
   C. A human resources requirement
   D. A tax requirement

Info:
A is the correct answer. If the customer has to require it, it is therefore not likely required by law (otherwise it would be provided without the customer requiring it). It could therefore be necessary for the performance of a contract but is likely not a legal obligation.

77. When processing personal data, certain things are required. Which of the following is not necessarily required?
   A. **A privacy notice (correct)**
   B. A lawful processing criterion
   C. A response to a data subject's request
   D. Records of processing activities

Info:
A is the correct answer. The information that needs to be provided specified in Articles 12 and 13 of the GDPR does not necessarily have to come in the form of a privacy notice. It is generally referred to as a privacy notice, but the form in which to provide it is free (as long as it meets the requirements of Articles 12 and 13).

78. An employee has access to files she was not supposed to access. Which of the following is most likely true?
    A. Since the access was within the organization, it is not a data breach
    B. As soon as the access is discovered, the extent of the access and consequences need to be assessed (correct)
    C. Due to the internal leak, the original lawful processing criterion cannot be relied on anymore
    D. Unless the employee shares the data, there is no data breach

Info:

B is the correct answer. In order to determine whether the situation constitutes a data breach, it needs to be assessed what exactly happened and what the consequences are. If the employee had access but never used it, the consequences are minimal and it perhaps does not constitute a data breach.

79. In case of a data breach, which of the following data processing principles is least likely violated?
    A. Confidentiality
    B. Proportionality (correct)
    C. Storage limitation
    D. Purpose limitation

Info:

B is the correct answer. A data breach is not likely the intention of the controller. It can therefore not be considered that the controller processed it or transferred it. Confidentiality is definitely breached, the storage will be exceeded, and it is used beyond the purpose for which it was collected. This, again, is a question where you need to follow the logic intended, which can be difficult (if not impossible).

This information can be used for the following four questions:

The data protection authority of one of the member states is conducting an investigation. An organization reported a data breach that potentially resulted in the loss of sensitive personal data of many data subjects.

After the organization suspected that the data was accessible by third parties due to the server configuration, it reported the incident to the data protection authority directly. At this moment the organization is only aware of there having been a possibility for outsiders to access the personal data (some of which was sensitive), and not whether it actually has been accessed or by whom.

The data protection authority found the incident shocking, regardless of whether personal data has been accessed by external parties. Because of that, they started an investigation.

80. The organization reported a data breach without knowing whether an external party accessed personal data. What is legally required of a controller?
    A. A data breach needs to be reported only if sensitive personal data has leaked
    B. Only if adverse consequences for the data subjects manifest themselves does a data breach need to be reported
    C. Only if a data subject complains does the organization need to report the data breach
    D. **A data breach needs to be reported without undue delay (correct)**

Info:
D is the correct answer. Article 33 (1) of the GDPR specifies that the controller needs to report a data breach "without undue delay". What undue delay means depends on the situation, so you will need to use common sense to determine whether the controller reported it without unnecessarily delaying.

81. In this case, what likely has the highest priority of the organization?
    A. The organization should perform background checks on employees
    B. The organization should figure out which personal data has been accessed by external parties (correct)
    C. Purchase a new firewall
    D. Purchase a better virus scanner

Info:

B is the correct answer. The size of the possible data breach needs to be figured out so the organization can take action. This could, for example, be to inform data subjects so that the data subjects can take action. Think of blocking a credit card if a list of credit card numbers has been leaked.

82. During its investigation, the data protection authority found that the storage on the server was not covered in the organization's data processing inventory. Who is likely held accountable for this?
    A. The organization's CEO (correct)
    B. The organization's CIO
    C. The organization's data protection officer
    D. The organization's privacy officer

Info:

A is the correct answer. The CEO is ultimately responsible, therefore also accountable. Whenever you encounter a question about responsibility or accountability, and you don't know the answer, pick the highest level of management.

83. For storing the personal data, what is most likely the lawful processing criterion the organization relies on?
    A. Legitimate interest
    B. The same lawful processing criterion the organization relied on for the collection (correct)
    C. Necessary for a contract
    D. Consent

Info:
B is the correct answer. There is no specific lawful processing criterion here, but it is likely the same one relied on for the collection. For example, if a controller needs certain personal data for the performance of a contract, it will need to collect it for the performance of that contract and to store it (for the time needed) for the performance of that contract.

84. An organization finds out it stores personal data since before the GDPR. Which of the following is most likely true?
    A. A new lawful processing criterion is necessary after May 25th 2018
    B. A new lawful processing criterion is necessary after May 25th 2016
    C. The same lawful processing criterion relied on under Directive 95 can be relied on (correct)
    D. Whether action needs to be taken depends on whether Binding Corporate Rules are in place

Info:
C is the correct answer. The lawful processing criteria of Directive 95 are similar to the lawful processing criteria of the GDPR. Although it cannot be said with 100% certainty, it logically follows that it is likely the same lawful processing criterion under the GDPR as under Directive 95.

85. A travel agency uses its customers' e-mail addresses for contacting them. Which of the following is the least possible?
    A. The contacting is in line with the collection purpose
    B. The data subject has opted in
    C. **The data subject has opted out (correct)**
    D. The data subject provided consent

Info:

C is the correct answer. If the contact via e-mail is needed for contacting the customers, that is different than marketing e-mails. Therefore, the opt-out requirement is not applicable. This does not mean that the travel agency does not use opt-out, because if there are other means of contacting the customers the travel agency could still provide an option to opt-out (and indicate that the travel agency should contact them only by phone, for example).

86. Which of the following is true regarding consent and the design of the processing of personal data?
    A. The process can continue if consent turns out to practically be irreversible
    B. There needs to be a privacy notice with a point of contact for withdrawing consent
    C. **The Privacy by Design principles likely result in the reversibility of consent at the earliest possible moment (correct)**
    D. Consent for the whole processing is implied if certain parts are optional to achieve the purpose

Info:

C is the correct answer. Privacy by Design should lead to as much privacy as possible due to taking privacy into account in each step of the design. Reversing consent as early as possible (so directly after the data subject retracts his/her consent) would be the most possible privacy of the available options. Option B is also correct but does not pertain to the design of the processing.

87. A logistics company's vehicles all send out maintenance indicators and connect with the company and other cars through the internet. This makes scheduling maintenance and planning pickups easier. What is this an example of?
    A. Software as a Service
    B. Biometric processing
    C. The Internet of Things (correct)
    D. IP tracking

Info:

C is the correct answer. The internet of things pertains to devices with sensors/indicators (etc.) communicating with each other (over the internet). This situation fits that definition.

88. When it concerns the international processing of personal data, when is a controller least likely required to have Binding Corporate Rules or a data processing agreement in place?
    A. A transfer within the organization
    B. A transfer to a non-processor third party (correct)
    C. When it concerns data processed by a processor in an adequate country
    D. An organization that does not process sensitive personal data

Info:

B is the correct answer. When a controller transfers to a third party, in this case, the third party is a controller. This means that the third party should be allowed to process the personal data, and the initial controller should be allowed to transfer the personal data to the third party. If these conditions are met, no agreements or rules need to be in place. Think of transferring financial data of your employees to the government tax agency, for example, which needs no agreement of any kind with the government tax agency.

89. A recruitment agency contacts you regarding a job opening. In which of the following cases is the recruitment agency least likely to rely on the lawful processing criterion legitimate interest?

A. When using the function of a social media website that allows recruiters to contact people with a certain profile (correct)

B. When browsing social media websites for suitable contacts and contacting them

C. Going through the database of CVs scraped from job searching websites

D. When a potential job applicant is in contact with the recruitment agency for another job

Info:

A is the correct answer. If you chose to use a feature on a social media website that allows recruiters to contact you, you have likely consented to the processing. Therefore, the lawful processing criterion is likely consent (depending on the details of the consent, of course).

90. When an organization uses an employee's personal e-mail address to reach the employee when the employee is on vacation, with a message that is not considered urgent, which of the data processing principles is most likely violated?

A. Proportionality (correct)

B. Accuracy

C. Storage limitation

D. Integrity

Info:

A is the correct answer. Contacting an employee away from work for something that is not urgent (and therefore likely not part of his/her job description/requirements), is likely not proportional.

Made in the USA
Las Vegas, NV
15 January 2024

84412579R00125